Praise for Tom Walker's
Building the Alaska Log Home

"A celebration of wilderness living . . . a good introduction to pioneering in the Northwoods."

—*Library Journal*

"I doubt there is another book in the market that would inspire one to build like this one does."

—Vic Janzen, Author, Log Builder

"The author carefully avoids the usual log home fantasy hype. He makes it sound like the hard work it is."

—*CoEvolution Quarterly*

". . . Stands head and shoulders over anything I've ever seen on the subject of log building."

—*Anchorage Daily News*

"If you've ever labored at building a log cabin—or thought it might be nice to build a cabin of your own—then this is the book for you."

—*Fairbanks Daily News-Miner*

"Not only is it informational, but interesting reading and inspiring."

—*Bridgewater Workshop North*

Building the Alaska Log Home

Tom Walker

ALASKA NORTHWEST BOOKS™

Anchorage ▪ Seattle ▪ Portland

First edition 1984
Second edition 1998

Library of Congress Cataloging-in-Publication Data:
Walker, Tom, 1945 –
    Building the Alaska log home / Tom Walker. — Rev. ed.
       p.   cm.
   ISBN 0-88240-511-X
   1. Log cabins—Design and construction.   2. Log cabins—Alaska—
Design and construction—History.   I. Title.
TH4840.W34   1998
690'.873—dc21   98-18123
                                                 CIP

Editors: Jim Rearden (1st ed.), Ellen Wheat (2nd ed.)
Cover Design: Elizabeth Watson
Interior Design: Jon.Hersh
Illustrations: Jon.Hersh, except as noted
Composition: Fay Bartels
Photographs by Tom Walker, except as noted

Alaska Northwest Books™
An imprint of Graphic Arts Center Publishing Company
P.O. Box 10306
Portland, OR 97296-0306
800-452-3032

Printed on acid-free paper in Hong Kong

Prologue

Since *Building the Alaska Log Home* was first published in 1984, some of the builders featured in this book have gone on to other occupations or have passed away. Derek Stonorov now makes custom high-concept hardwood furniture; master builders Paul Smith and Lee Cole passed away. Other builders, like Jimmy Hitchcock and Art Mannix, keep on building. Also, some of the homes shown in the book have changed ownership.

The craft of log building has matured, each builder adding innovations and perfecting technique. A log home *is* a slice of old-growth forest—this book still offers the basic concepts and how to use logs with respect and care.

Denali Park, 1998

The covered porch to Brian Okonek's wilderness retreat, which is built from dead-standing timber. Note the way the logs are peeled and the burl truss over the door.

Contents

Preface

Designed for the neophyte cabin builder, this book details, step by step, the construction of log buildings, complete from turning trees into logs to the first fire in the wood stove. Professional logsmiths throughout Alaska provided material and inspiration for this book. Although no two logsmiths build exactly alike or agree on all things, this compendium, assembled for the novice, reflects a general consensus. Based on the professionals' techniques and secrets, the text, diagrams, and photos will help most anyone build a warm, comfortable log cabin.

Let's get one thing straight from the beginning: log building means hard work, very hard work. Somewhere along the line you may think you've been sentenced to a term at hard labor and start looking for shortcuts, but there just isn't any substitute for hard work, sweat, and patience. Take the time to do it right. The rewards may not be apparent at first, but they will be later on. From peeling logs to setting the ridgepole, each day means hard labor. That's the price.

This is a good time to dismantle a few other myths, too. Log cabins aren't necessarily warmer than conventional frame structures. And log buildings definitely are not cheaper to build than a frame building of equal size, and they take much more time to complete.

Well, then, if logwork takes longer, costs more, isn't always warmer, and is such hard work, why build with logs? Two simple reasons: practicality and aesthetics. In some remote areas, logs remain the only practical building materials. Dimensional lumber costs a fortune to purchase

I built this unique L-shaped home for Mike and Linda Gephardt. The logwork—round-notch, chinkless construction—took me almost three months. The roof design and construction was done by William E. Ruth. Still to be added is a Swiss porch above the front door. Note the settling spaces above the door and windows.

In late autumn one year I built this small V-plank-corner cabin with frame gables for Will and Lurue Troyer near the old Juneau Lake Trail on the Kenai Peninsula.

and transport, so some builders must use local materials. In more developed areas, the aesthetic appeal of logs and handcraftsmanship far outweigh the higher dollar cost of log construction. That's not to say that cabins in remote areas don't reflect the builder's aesthetics; rather, the cabin there rises out of necessity, while elsewhere, solely because of artistic appeal. A log building is *the* personalized statement of the builder. A work of art. No two will ever be the same.

By now it should be apparent that in this book I will not be discussing rude or temporary shelters but, rather, permanent, sturdy structures. We live in a largely synthetic world. Fakery abounds. Most wood-finish products are imitation or thin veneer. Homes made from aluminum and synthetics house people sick of the sterility of carbon-copy dwellings. Each year more people escape to genuine wood homes, and for those most in tune with the natural world, log homes. A log home is a genuinely handcrafted, one-of-a-kind creation. Nothing can compare to the beauty and grace of a well-built log cabin, blending with its surroundings as if it had grown from the soil. And nothing, absolutely nothing, can compare to the satisfaction of knowing you built it!

Old cabins, whether occupied, vacant, or collapsed, do something to me. They have a definite aura. Whether I'm inside, or outside standing and staring, or stepping through ruins, a certain feeling overwhelms me. Hard to describe, really. Almost a depression, but no, more. A melancholy. In the occupied ones, the cabins well-built and loved, a genuine and full appreciation grips me. I grow quiet as I think of the living that went on there and the times past. I admire the craftsmanship, the permanence of logs maintained and respected. In the abandoned ones, questions overwhelm my appreciation: Why is this cabin vacant? My feeling changes to a vague sadness, loneliness really. This cold loneliness grows strongest in the unexpected discovery of the skeletal rubble of a decaying cabin overtaken with brush.

Who built it? And why? Why did they leave? What's left? A post-mortem inevitably ensues. Where did the design fail?

Why did the walls buckle inward? Why did the builder spend so much, or so little, time here? Endless. In all cases, it's almost as if the cabin had a spirit of its own. Who's to say no? Weren't these living trees once? Maybe for some of us, I know I'm not alone, the spirit of those who lived here, mingled with tree spirits, lingers on, reaches out. Or maybe it's just the empathy of a builder for another's handiwork.

In Alaska there are plenty of old cabins, plenty of opportunities to encounter these definite vibrations. Alaskan history boils with fabulous epics. When Russian fur hunters first came into the country seeking sea otter and fur seal, ermine and sable (marten), a wealth of timber provided logs for their strong and sturdy buildings: forts, blockhouses, and defendable billets and churches. With broadax and adz they hewed and fit logs in grand style. These were the first cabins in Alaska, and they were built to last. The Russian handiwork can still be viewed today in Kodiak, Sitka, Fort Kenay (Kenai), and elsewhere.

Alaska's wealth brought others north—traders, explorers, whalers, sealers, and gold stampeders. These came to stay but awhile, and many built poorly, if at all. Quality log cabins were then a rarity, with slipshod the rule. All sizes and types of cabins went up, with logs joined in a variety of styles. Most of the gold rush–era cabins lasted less than 20 years, though a few of the better ones still remain.

In 1899, Major P. H. Ray, a veteran Alaskan explorer, led his troops to Fort Egbert at Eagle, on the Alaska-Yukon border, to build a post and help establish law and order.

In the central Brooks Range near Poss Mountain, I came upon this rotting skeleton of a small cabin, its sod roof collapsed inward. In awe I thought of the man who had spent a winter on that frozen watershed at subzero temperatures in months of complete darkness.

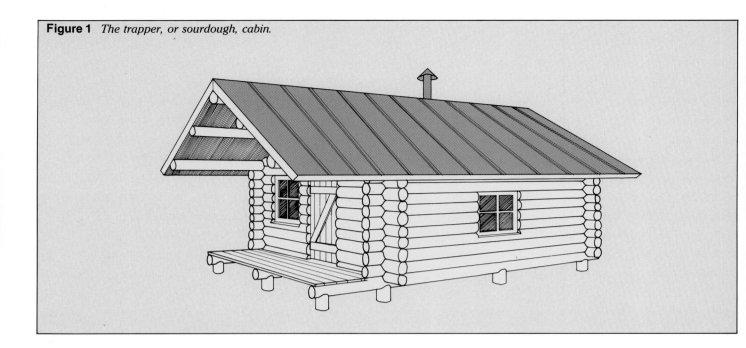

Figure 1 *The trapper, or sourdough, cabin.*

After his arrival, construction of log buildings and barracks continued apace, yet a young soldier's diary entry written that following winter, when the mercury plunged to -60° F, tells much about the quality of those log buildings: "The cracks in the logs let in the Alaskan climate faster than we could drive it out with a stove in each room."

A log cabin need not be crude or short-lived; indeed, should not be. In Norway, log buildings still in use today have stood for more than 600 years. The early demise of pioneer cabins makes a sad commentary on those who came North for but a short time.

Many of the old cabins, other than those of Russian origin, seem to have been designed by the same person. They are functional rectangular boxes. Well built or poor, most have low walls and a low-pitched pole-and-sod roof. Some have two purlins and one ridgepole; others, two purlins on either side of the ridgepole. Some even have a double ridgepole. All were designed to retain as much heat as possible. Some did, others didn't. I call this simple, basic design the trapper, or sourdough, cabin (Figure 1). As a learning example, this

design, with modifications, is featured in this book.

One of three principal design features, or combinations thereof, contributed to the early demise of most old collapsed cabins: the foundation, the corner notches, and/or the sod roof. Obviously a foundation is important. Logs in contact with the soil just don't last. Poorly constructed notches let the moisture accumulate and attack the wood fiber. And the sod roof, though quaint and very Alaskan, proves anathema to those wanting a cabin to last. All too often, roof boards and supporting logs give way to the ravages of moisture absorbed by the sod. Some old cabins with their roofs collapsed otherwise look well built, the foundations and notches done with care.

In this book, I give details on all important and unique aspects of building with logs. Emphasis is also on alternate forms of construction techniques, techniques workable in remote or wilderness areas. Hopefully, if you build carefully, 50 or 60 years from now someone will look on your handiwork, not with sadness or scorn, but with admiration and respect for the old skills well-employed.

Gary Rogers built this home for his wife and family on the edge of the Kenai River. He used both two-sided logs, which he slabbed himself, and three-sided logs. The bench on the porch was made from milled spruce rounds.

Part One

Wouldn't it be great to build a cabin employing just hand tools? Gimlet, adz, ax, crosscut. Just like the old days. No noxious fumes or noise from a chainsaw. No expensive gas and oil. Only the steady *chip-chip-chip* of cutting tools. Man in harmony with his work. Recently a friend did just that— built his log home with hand tools. Without a doubt, it is one of the best-crafted cabins I've ever seen. The only drawback is that it took almost three years to build.

If time means nothing and you have the desire, by all means use hand tools. It would be a delight, but few folks seem to have that kind of time; I never do. Using a chainsaw, my friend could have built his cabin in three months instead of three years, and the quality would not have suffered.

Chainsaws use gasoline, pollute the air (fumes and noise), and can be dangerous to operate. But to a professional logsmith, they're beauty. Using one, a person with even limited ability can build, furnish, and fuel a home. A good chainsaw costs plenty, but will compensate by saving time and energy. The *chip-chip-chip* of hand tools might have its atavistic appeal, but for the last 20 years, the sound of power saws screaming like 40-pound bees has accompanied logwork.

In 1926, Andreas Stihl, a German, invented the chainsaw. Over the years Stihl refined his basic design, trimming the ponderous, original two-man saw down to one-man size, thereby revolutionizing logging. In principle, the original design remains much the same today, with well over two million saws, built by several manufacturers, sold annually in the United States. Homelite, McCulloch, Pioneer, Poulan, Partner,

Tools

Traditional hand tools—whipsaw, crosscut saw, drawknife, block, hatchet, broadax, mallet, ax, auger, and a broken brace—hang on the side of Harold Eastwood's cabin.

Although master logsmiths such as Paul Smith of Cooper Landing often use a double-bitted ax to chop out a notch, a beginner would be wiser not to—it is too easy to make a misstroke and ruin the work.

Skil, Echo, Husqvarna, Remington, Stihl, and others, offer more than 200 models to choose from. From that bewildering array, which is best for the log builder?

The ideal cabin builder's saw has a modest price tag, uses little gas, makes no noise, doesn't pollute the air, and is light and easy to use. A saw like this hasn't been made, but some come close. Most any quality lightweight-duty chainsaw, in the 9- to 13.5-pound category, equipped with a 16- to 20-inch bar, preferably 16-inch, will do the job. Much depends on the user and the care given the saw. Many logsmiths use several saws, professional application sometimes requiring big, powerful saws as well as small, specialized ones.

If your intent is to build one cabin and not go into professional tree felling or logsmithing, select a saw for a variety of chores, such as cutting firewood, clearing brush, and felling small trees. The light-weight-duty saws fill the bill; mini-saws do not. And heavyweight-duty saws are just too skookum for the once-in-a-lifetime builder—they are far and away too much saw for around-home use. Buy the best-quality saw you can afford, but just remember, bigger isn't always better. Match the saw to your needs.

My personal favorite for notching and for most building chores comes with an automatic oiler, a roller tip, and a 16-inch bar. At 13 pounds dry, it's not too heavy even at the end of the work day, and the balance and simplicity make it an ideal logsmithing tool. I also use a larger saw, a Jonsered 630 with a 24-inch bar, for cutting windows, doors, and gables, and for some trim work.

Chainsaw salesmen tell us that chainsaws are not inherently dangerous. I suppose, semantically anyway, that's correct. Such statements, however, depend on one's definition of dangerous. For example, in 1982, 123,000 persons were injured, some fatally, in chainsaw accidents. And as the demand for firewood increases, and saw sales climb, the numbers may grow as well. A chainsaw can cut through a log in a matter of seconds, so it should be no surprise that it can cut through an arm or leg in a split second. Chains can break and whip back viciously at the operator. Combined with a phenomenon called kickback, these aspects make a chainsaw a tool to operate carefully, never carelessly. See Figure 2 below.

Slightly less than 40% of all chainsaw accidents result from kickback. Every user of a chainsaw should know about kickback, what causes it, and how to avoid it. Kickback occurs when the chain hangs up—stops—coming around the upper tip of the bar, the kickback zone. If the chain there contacts and catches on a solid object—wood, rock, ground, or whatever—it stops for a split second; but the engine is still under power and something has to give. The reaction is a violent rotation backward of the chainsaw, with the now-speeding chain whipping back at the operator.

Kickback can be somewhat controlled with mini-saws operated properly; rarely on lightweight saws; and never on heavyweights. Of all the injuries sustained by professional timber fallers, 38% resulted from kickback. Obviously, even a strong person isn't powerful enough to control the backward swipe of the saw.

Manufacturers are constantly developing and upgrading safety features. An anti-kickback device, called the chain brake, is standard equipment on most models. *First-time chainsaw users and novice log builders should not even consider using a chainsaw that is not equipped with a chain brake.* A chain brake is a mechanical device intended

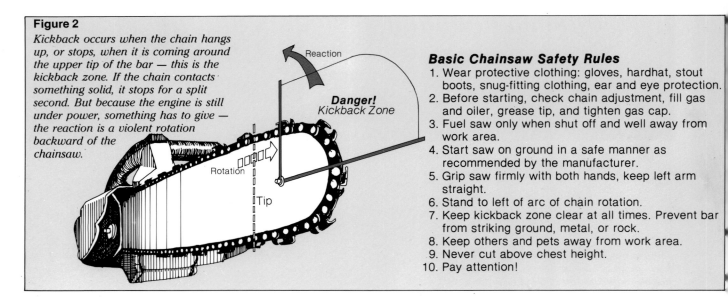

Figure 2

Kickback occurs when the chain hangs up, or stops, when it is coming around the upper tip of the bar — this is the kickback zone. If the chain contacts something solid, it stops for a split second. But because the engine is still under power, something has to give — the reaction is a violent rotation backward of the chainsaw.

Reaction

Danger!
Kickback Zone

Rotation

Tip

Basic Chainsaw Safety Rules
1. Wear protective clothing: gloves, hardhat, stout boots, snug-fitting clothing, ear and eye protection.
2. Before starting, check chain adjustment, fill gas and oiler, grease tip, and tighten gas cap.
3. Fuel saw only when shut off and well away from work area.
4. Start saw on ground in a safe manner as recommended by the manufacturer.
5. Grip saw firmly with both hands, keep left arm straight.
6. Stand to left of arc of chain rotation.
7. Keep kickback zone clear at all times. Prevent bar from striking ground, metal, or rock.
8. Keep others and pets away from work area.
9. Never cut above chest height.
10. Pay attention!

to stop the chain, or chain and power plant, in the event the saw kicks back. Most brakes are operated by a lever mounted ahead of the saw's handle and brakes the chain at the moment of kickback. Safety experts conclude that while power-saw use represents potential safety hazards, those who use saws with chain brakes stand the best chance of reducing risk. Since January 1981, Canadian Safety Standard has required all gas-powered chainsaws sold in Canada to be equipped with chain brakes.

Homelite developed and distributes a simple, one-piece guard, the Safe-T-Tip, that bolts to the bar and shields the kickback zone. This attachment effectively eliminates kickback. Used while felling, limbing, or bucking, the Safe-T-Tip provides exceptional protection from kickback but, unfortunately, usually gets in the way when cutting notches. Another safety development is the low-profile chain, also called the three-eighths mini-chipper, or low-

kick chain. Because the low-profile chain doesn't attack the wood as aggressively, it is less likely to kick back.

Chains come in all lengths and styles. For the builder, the most useful are the standard chipper chain and the ripper chain. The chipper is adaptable to all kinds of timber and cutting conditions and comes as original equipment on most saws. The ripping chain provides a fast, smooth-ripping cut, ideal for use with the various chainsaw lumber-making mills.

Though a saw can be dangerous, many logsmiths have worked 10 or 20 years without sustaining kickback injuries. I have built 10 cabins in the last seven years and have experienced kickback a time or two, but because of constant awareness and safety precautions, I have avoided injury. Alertness, plus the chain brake or Safe-T-Tip, is the user's most reliable protection from kickback.

Chains should be kept as sharp as

possible. Each morning before work, as well as at intervals throughout the day, when you clean the chainsaw, fill the oiler and gas tank, and grease the rotating tip, sharpen your saw. A dull saw cuts inefficiently and imprecisely, and because you use the tip a lot in logwork, chains dull quickly. In addition, a dull saw will not cut a straight line, which is especially important when cutting window and door openings. Also, mill attachments won't help you much if the chain is dull. Use the appropriate chainsaw file or round file, not a rattail file, as specified by the manufacturer.

Although with a little experience most folks can sharpen a dull chain using an adjustable file holder/guide, it takes quite a bit more experience to get it perfect. Sometimes it is essential to have an accurate, like-new chain. The File-N-Joint clamp-on chainsaw sharpener by Granberg Industries, the makers of the Alaskan MK III chainsaw mill, makes most anyone with the ability

Slabbed with an MK III mill, this log will serve as the first wall log on a large house. The milled side will go down against the platform and the log will be bolted to the foundation.

This is a good illustration of how the Alaskan MK III chainsaw can be used to mill bearing surfaces on logs. Here Paul McArthur is using a Stihl saw to slab a log. The safety helmet affords good hearing protection. Note the guide rail for the saw and attachment and the auxiliary oiler mounted on the attachment.

Tool Check List

Get the best-quality tools you can afford, always with an eye to future use. Most tools on this list are basic carpentry items and can be used for many and varied projects. Many of the options can be very helpful, but may not be absolutely necessary.

___ Chainsaw (9 to 13.5 pounds)
___ Scribe (wing, or extension dividers)
___ Drawknife (13- to 14-inch blade)
___ Hudson Bay ax
___ Peavey (42 to 47 inches)
___ Come-along (hand winch)
___ Chainsaw file and guide
___ Approved gas can, funnel
___ File or stone for ax
___ Steel tapes (12-foot and 50-foot)
___ Hammer (16-ounce)
___ Sledge hammer (short handle)
___ Steel square
___ Chalkbox, line, and chalk
___ String line and line level
___ Level (24-inch)
___ Firmer socket chisel (1$\frac{1}{2}$ to 2 inches, heavy-duty)
___ Bit and brace or power drill
___ Bits: ship augers ($\frac{5}{8}$-inch and 1-inch; overall length 17 inches; twist length 12 inches)

___ Crosscut handsaw (10-point)
___ Ripsaw (4$\frac{1}{2}$-point)
___ Chainsaw tool
___ Plastic wedges
___ Safety clothing, helmet, eye and ear protection
___ Haddon Lumber/Maker

Options
___ Broadax
___ Slick
___ Log dogs
___ Adz
___ Block and tackle
___ Disc sander
___ Bark spud
___ Granberg File-N-Joint
___ Alaskan MK III chainsaw mill

Sources of Tools

Northern Hardware
P.O. Box 1499
Burnsville, MN 55337
1-800-222-5381

Woodworker's Supply
1108 North Glenn Road
Casper, WY 82601
1-800-645-9292

WoodCraft Supply
P.O. Box 1686
Parkersburg, WV 26102-1686
1-800-225-1153

Bailey's (Western Division)
P.O. Box 550
Laytonville, CA 95454
1-800-322-4539

Cutter's Choice
2008 East Third Street
Erie, PA 16514
1-800-824-8521

Veritas Tools Inc.
12 East River Street
Ogdensburg, NY 13669
or
1080 Morrison Drive
Ottawa, ON K2A 8K7
Canada

Log building tools. Front row from left: 50-foot tape, 12-foot tape, chalkbox, ax file, chisel, felling wedge, saw file and guide, hammer, hand sledge, and chainsaw. Middle row from left: auger bits and torpedo level. Back row from left: broadax, peavey, adz, Hudson Bay ax (handle is taped for a good grip, not because it is broken!), and slick. On the wall from left: log dogs, ear protectors, come-along, and drawknife.

Here I have been sanding the interior of a cabin built of fire-killed logs. A wise person would sand the logs first, before placing them on the wall. Use only a heavy-duty disc sander and always wear eye and ear protectors and a respirator mask.

to read directions a chain-sharpening expert. This device turns out a precision-sharp chain, and is an excellent investment.

A couple of chainsaw attachments prove invaluable to logsmiths. The Alaskan MK III chainsaw mill has unlimited application. This high-quality, advanced-design, clamp-on lumbermill converts rough logs into slabs or perfectly dimensioned lumber in thicknesses from 1 inch to 12 inches. Many logsmiths use the MK III to cut their own two-sided logs, while others use it to mill floor joists, rafters, and bearing surfaces on caplogs, purlins, and ridgepole. However, the MK III is expensive and may be too big an investment for the one-time builder.

Another device, the Haddon Lumber/Maker, is affordable and useful, and should be in every builder's tool box. Simple, efficient, fast, and easy to use, the Lumber/Maker makes all kinds of lumber and is an invaluable aid for cutting window and door openings and trimming the gable ends. The Lumber/Maker attaches to the bar with three set screws. Using a guide board nailed to a log or wall, the tool guides the saw for accurate, straight cuts.

One last caution about chainsaws: *Always* wear hearing protection. Running a saw all day is harmful to your hearing. Shooter's-style earmuffs or plugs offer good protection. Use them. Manufacturers have done wonders the last few years producing ever-quieter chainsaw designs, but hearing is precious. Once it's gone, it's gone. The same is true of eyesight, too, so I recommend safety glasses.

Many logsmiths swear by the Hudson Bay–style ax. This three-quarter-size ax gives all the value of a full-size ax but with half the weight, usually less than 3 pounds. The flat head can pound pegs or drive nails, and the wide cutting blade can hew logs or limb trees. Still other logsmiths use nothing but double-bitted axes (but obviously don't drive nails with them) or stouter competition axes.

A broadax, also called broad hatchet or side ax, has been used since frontier days to hand-hew logs. If you are using only hand tools, this one is a necessity for hewing logs, rafters, joists, and bearing surfaces. Many early Alaskan cabins were built with squared logs hewn with broadaxes.

Nothing is more worthless than a dull ax. They gouge or glance off wood instead of cutting in cleanly. I use a file to sharpen my axes; others use a stone, or both a file and stone. Whatever you use, keep your axes sharp for clean cuts and for safety's sake.

Drawknives come with blade lengths of from 5 to 14 inches. Essential to logsmithing, this tool should be chosen carefully. The ideal drawknife, with tang ends that extend completely through large wooden handles, has a blade 13 to 14 inches long and 2 inches wide. Such a knife will handle the toughest job. Europeans, as well as American producers, still make drawknifes at prices varying from $60 to $95.

A drawknife should be kept sharp, too. Bark comes off dry logs only with vigorous effort. Cutting or pulling the drawknife against knots only dulls it. Peel bark and wood with the drawknife and use the ax to remove knots and limbs. Keep your knees out of the way when peeling hard-to-remove bark. Should the knife slip, or the bark give way suddenly, the knife will end up in your knee, or peeling your kneecap. Only an expert can properly sharpen a drawknife. Take it to one.

A bark spud, which looks like an ice chipper but with a curved cutting head, is used by cabin builders to strip bark from freshly cut logs. It can be a useful tool, but the drawknife is better and faster, especially on dried-on bark.

A socket slick has been used for centuries by carpenters, boatwrights, and log builders to level hand-hewn surfaces and clean up large mortises, and for other paring jobs. It is especially useful for edging the scribe line on full-scribe logs.

Log dogs are the clamps for the logsmith and timber framer. One end is driven into the log and the other into the building or supporting log. In this way the log being worked on is held firmly in place.

Another worthwhile cutting tool is the adz, sometimes wryly called the toe-hoe. Applied in the manner of a hoe, the adz earned its nickname by sometimes

Drawknives are essential to log building. After I finished smoothing this milled log, it became a second-story floor joist.

(John Szajkowski)

Use an adz to hollow out the lateral groove on scribe-fit logs. Scoring cuts are made between the scribe lines so that wood sections will pop out with the blow of the adz.

A log dog will hold a log in place while a notch is being fashioned; note the peavey in the background. Also note the bolt through the log in the foreground— the tar around the bolt is to prevent water from soaking through the auger hole during construction.

glancing off wood and into the toe or shin of the user. This time-honored tool can be used to hollow notches, or cup the lateral groove on scribe-fit logs.

You will need a bit and brace or heavy-duty electric drill to drill the logs for rebar or pegs. By far, the best bits to use are ship's augers.

One almost irreplaceable, work-saving tool useful for prying and turning logs is the peavey. Designed as a modified cant hook in 1857 by Joseph Peavey, a Maine blacksmith, this tool basically serves as a heavy-duty lever with an attached fulcrum. I well remember time spent wrestling logs in the bush without a peavey, and I'll never be without one again.

A 7½-pound cable and ratchet hoist puller, called a come-along or hand winch, commonly available in one-ton or two-ton capacity, can also be an indispensable aid in moving logs. I always seem to end up building cabins alone, and this tool, with the exception of the chainsaw, has proved the most valuable. I've even moved logs to the site, a crank at a time, and set a ridgepole high off the ground with just a come-along for help.

No professional logsmith worth his salt would be without his scribe. This tool, unique to log building, is invaluable for making accurate notches and for scribe-fitting logs. A scribe can be a simple unadorned carpenter's or machinist's dividers (they look like a child's school compass), or a more complex, one-of-a-kind creation, but it is absolutely essential to log building.

Many fine cabins with tight-fitting notches have been built with the aid of ordinary dividers. The dividers are used to carefully transcribe the shape of the lower log onto the upper log, indicating the area to be cut away for the notch. (See Chapter Six for complete details.)

For perfect joinery, affix a small level at right angles to the upper leg of the dividers. While scribing the notch, you can center the bubble and keep the tool perfectly level, thus ensuring accuracy. A level attachment makes most anyone an expert.

Scribes get more complicated when it comes to scribe-fit, also called Scandinavian, or chinkless, log construction. These scribes have two levels, at right angles to each other, mounted on the upper divider leg. The levels are used to make absolutely certain the scribe line will be perfect and plumb to the corresponding points on the log below. If the scribe is tipped, right or left or up or down, the level bubbles indicate the variation, and the correction can be made accordingly.

Many logsmiths who build with the full-scribe technique make their own scribes (somewhat tricky, as levels must be adjustable, since every scribe setting differs and the angle to the levels change). Others buy scribes. Mine was built for me to my specifications, out of a wing divider and part of a gun barrel, by Tom Mantzoros, a machinist and custom gunsmith.

Derek Stonorov using a commercially available scribe to scribe a lateral groove.

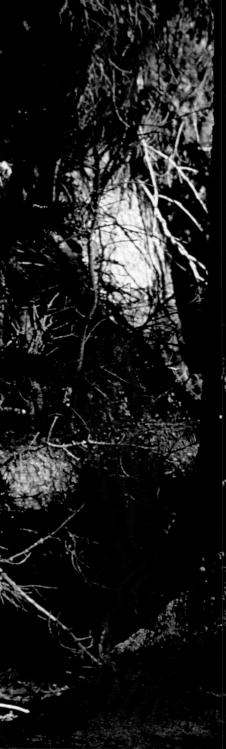

T rees — nature's largest and most successful creation. Some stand hundreds of feet high and weigh up to half a million pounds. On the Nevada-California border are the bristlecone pines, the oldest living things. I've hiked up to look at them. Stunted and twisted by the wind, they don't look like much, but some have been living since before Christ.

The trees that go into a cabin won't be the biggest or the oldest, and they definitely won't be gnarled, but they will be old, many of them 150 to 200 years old. Think about it as you work. It took a long time for that tree to grow and it's your responsibility as the cabin builder to use it wisely.

Nature blessed North America with a wealth of tree species. Since earliest settler days, spruce, balsam, fir, tamarack, hemlock, cedar, and redwood,

A near-perfect alignment of back cut and directional cut. A wedge driven into the back cut will cause the tree to topple in the desired direction.

plus such short-life woods as birch and aspen, have been used by cabin builders. Today we face many of the same problems in building a cabin that the pioneers did, including the most basic: cutting the trees and moving them to the site.

For many of us, cutting trees for a cabin is entirely out of the question. You can purchase logs from a mill, contract logger, lumberyard, or public agency. In some cases, buying logs will result in a higher-quality product since you can custom-order uniform-size logs.

Buying logs can't compare to the experience of logging your own, but unless the logging takes place on private property, you will need a permit, and in some areas, permits will not be issued at all. On U.S. Forest Service land, cutting green timber for house logs requires a permit issued under the terms of a noncompetitive timber sale contract. State, federal, and Native lands have different regulations. Check land ownership and permit requirements before cutting. The permit requires lead time, even bids in some areas; requires cleanup of slash and winter logging to minimize impact; sets

Timber into Logs

Tom Mantzoros makes the first cut in the process of felling a spruce. Tom's position is to the side of the direction of the fall, which will be directly toward the viewer. In addition to the hearing protection, Tom should be wearing a hard hat.

a fixed amount of time to haul out the logs; and prohibits the building of access roads.

You can, however, avoid all the permit hassles and cost by using dead-standing timber, usually fire-killed or beetle-killed trees. For example, in Alaska, a free Forest Service permit will allow you to use up to 10,000 board feet of dead-standing timber.

Besides being free, using dead stuff has many advantages and few disadvantages, although one obvious disadvantage is that not all dead-standing timber is suitable for house logs. Some defects, such as rotten centers or tops, won't show up until the tree is cut down. Some fire-killed trees require extensive drawknifing or power sanding to remove weathering or charring. For the most part, however, the advantages greatly outweigh these, and a few other, negative aspects.

First, and best of all, using dead timber means that no living trees are killed. The clearcutters do enough of that for us all. A dead-standing tree generally has few limbs to remove and

is easier to peel than a green tree with the bark dried on. In many cases, dead timber has dried out completely, a very important advantage, especially if you plan on hauling the logs yourself. A green white spruce log, Alaska's most common house log species, with a 14- to 16-inch butt and 30 to 40 feet long, will weigh 1,200 pounds or more. (The Forest Service weight estimate is 33 pounds per cubic foot.) A dry log that size might weigh one-third to one-half that.

If it is possible to harvest your own cabin logs, bear in mind that logging, with a death rate for professional tree fallers of 12.5 per 1,000 workers per year, ranks as the most dangerous occupation in the country. True, you won't be felling a 200-foot-tall, 250,000-pound giant, but a 60- or 70-foot spruce can kill you just as quickly as one of the giants.

Careful tree selection should be of obvious importance. Although with a little more work a quality cabin can be built from poor-quality logs, the best cabins are built with logs that are

straight and not tapered, that are undamaged by hauling or limbing, and that are of uniform size. The size of tree to fell depends on several factors: cabin size, method of transport, and overall availability of trees. Obviously, the bigger the logs, the fewer you need to reach wall height (which means less work) and the warmer the cabin (big logs keep the heat in). However, good logs with a butt size of more than 14 inches are hard to find in many sections of Alaska (see Figure 3).

In Alaska, the white spruce is the most common house log species. White spruce grow slowly and, in Interior Alaska for example, don't reach saw timber size for 100 to 500 years. White spruce grow best on south-facing slopes in well-drained soils, and even in Alaska's Interior reach heights of 80 feet or more. Interior Alaska is not thought of as an area of prime commercial forest, yet of Alaska's 28.2 million acres classed as commercial forest, 22.5 million acres are in the Interior, with an inventory estimate of 30.8 billion board feet. There, white spruce predominates over 12.8 million acres. Obviously, there is not a shortage of timber, but a shortage of accessible timber.

In coastal Alaska, the size of log most in demand is one 30 to 40 feet long with a 14- to 16-inch butt. Because white spruce tapers quickly, a log this size comes from a 70- to 80-foot tree. Farther north the log size gets smaller. A good-size log to work with is one with a midpoint size of 10 inches (butt of 12 inches).

Before planning your cabin, inventory the trees available for the project and plan accordingly. In some areas, the forest won't produce 30- to 40-foot logs without unacceptable bowing or tapering. To allow for notching and overhang, the logs must be 4 feet longer than the desired inside dimensions of the cabin. If the cabin's inside dimensions are 16 feet by 18 feet, the log sizes required are 20 feet and 22 feet. The caplogs (the last logs up on the side walls), the purlins, and the ridgepole must be even longer. On a 16-foot-by-18-foot cabin, these logs should be a minimum of 24 feet long. In some areas a 24-foot log is the

Figure 3   Alaska's Biggest Trees (1984)

Species	Circumference at 4.5 feet above ground	Estimated Diameter (feet)	Estimated Height (feet)	Location
Red alder	8 ft., 11 in.	2.8	53	Admiralty Island
Quaking aspen	5 ft., 6 in.	1.8	73	Near Northway
Paper birch	7 ft., 7 in.	2.4	55	Susitna Valley
Alaska cedar	27 ft., 9 in.	8.8	85	Hydaburg
Western red cedar	29 ft., 10 in.	9.5	105	Revillagigedo Island
Black cottonwood	32 ft., 6 in.	10.4	101	Klukwan
Douglas fir	4 ft., 5 in.	1.4	48	Near Ketchikan
Pacific silver fir	12 ft., 10 in.	4.1	148	Boca de Quadra
Subalpine fir	6 ft., 7 in.	2.1	95	Taku River
Mountain hemlock	12 ft., 1 in.	3.9	105	Chilkat Range
Western Hemlock	19 ft., 3 in.	6.1	150	Admiralty Island
Shore pine	9 ft., 3 in.	3.0	93	Prince of Wales Island
Balsam poplar	6 ft., 11 in.	2.2	60	Vinasale, Kuskokwim River
Black spruce	3 ft., 8 in.	1.2	65	Tolovana, Tanana River
Sitka spruce	29 ft., 10 in.	9.5	185	Prince of Wales Island
White spruce	8 ft., 1 in.	2.6	88	Williams Slough, Tanana River
Tamarack	3 ft., 5 in.	1.1	77	Mile 311, Richardson Hwy.
Pacific yew	2 ft., 6 in.	0.8	30	Dog Island, Southeastern

This list is kept updated by the U.S. Forest Service Forest Science Library in Juneau, Alaska.

maximum size available, but in others, two logs that size can be cut from one tree (although, obviously, they won't be of the same butt size).

A cheechako will not only find it hard to pick straight trees, but the right butt-size trees as well. For uniform results, measure each tree around the base before felling. Cut only trees of the same basal circumference. The circumference of a living tree will be greater than the actual building log size, since the bark must be peeled and some wood will be wasted as well. In most of Alaska, a tree with a 32-inch circumference will yield a building log with a 9-inch butt; a 38-inch circumference will yield an 11-inch butt; and a 40-inch circumference log, a 12-inch butt. (Don't bother trying to figure this out with the old formula circumference equals pi times diameter, because these figures take into account the bark and waste wood, while figuring a finished log diameter.) These are rough measurements that have proved to be fairly accurate for most boreal forests.

Select the tree for quality, size, and location. For the novice it's best to avoid cutting leaning trees and those that are in dense timber or on slopes. That can come with experience. Pick a straight tree (look closely; it isn't as easy as you might think) and one relatively in the open with a clear, unobstructed line of fall. A falling tree smashing into another can snap off at the top, possibly ruining a log or launching dangerous fragments into the air. A falling tree also can hang up in another. The work involved in removing it is great and the risk high. Also, before felling, look closely for a deadman or widowmaker, a dead or broken limb up high. A saw cutting into the tree can jar these loose. And finally, before cutting, clear an area around the base of the tree and identify an escape path at a 45-degree angle to the line of fall. Remember, even with a directional cut, it is still possible for the tree to fall opposite to the way you planned.

Make a directional cut (Figure 4) aimed toward the intended point of impact. Always stand beside the tree and away from the cut, making it as close to the ground as is feasible. The

Tom Mantzoros making the directional cut on a small spruce. Note his position to the side of the tree.

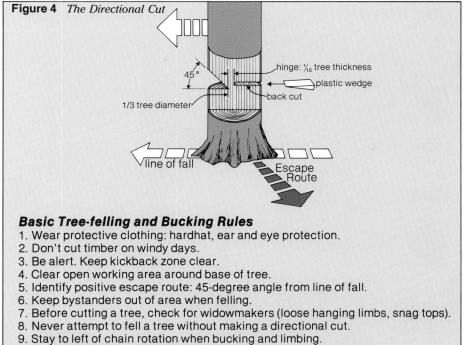

Figure 4   *The Directional Cut*

45°

hinge: 1/10 tree thickness

plastic wedge

back cut

1/3 tree diameter

line of fall

Escape Route

Basic Tree-felling and Bucking Rules
1. Wear protective clothing: hardhat, ear and eye protection.
2. Don't cut timber on windy days.
3. Be alert. Keep kickback zone clear.
4. Clear open working area around base of tree.
5. Identify positive escape route: 45-degree angle from line of fall.
6. Keep bystanders out of area when felling.
7. Before cutting a tree, check for widowmakers (loose hanging limbs, snag tops).
8. Never attempt to fell a tree without making a directional cut.
9. Stay to left of chain rotation when bucking and limbing.
10. Stand uphill when bucking; use wedges to prevent bar pinch.

Bill Hightower hauling a log from the
woods with his small tractor. Unless a
good road is available, something more
than a four-wheel-drive truck is needed to
move logs during the summer.

It's easier to move logs in the winter when
even a small recreational snowmobile can
be used. All you need is a go-devil and a
packed (and preferably level) trail to the
building site.

initial horizontal cut should be about one-third of the tree's diameter. Make the downcut to it at about a 45-degree angle. Remove this wedge of wood with the ax, not your hand. One sharp blow should do it. Now comes the back cut. This cut should be about 2 inches above the horizontal line of the directional cut. Saw into the tree until enough space has been made to accommodate both the saw and a plastic wedge. Stop the saw and lightly pound in a wedge. Make sure it is in the center of the cut and not touching the chain. This will help direct the fall and prevent the bar from being pinched. Start the saw and continue the back cut. Cut only to the hinge, then stop. The tree should start to fall. Remove the saw and get well away, following your planned escape route. If the tree doesn't fall when you reach hinge depth, don't cut through or past it. Remove the saw and drive the wedge in with the ax. The cracking sound will be the warning to get clear.

The sobering crash of the tree and the mini-earthquake following should impress you with the need for caution and safety.

Limb the tree carefully. Some folks use a chainsaw to do this. Don't you. The saw easily cuts into the trunk, marring it. Use the ax, cutting the limbs as close to the trunk as possible without gouging into the wood. Stand on the opposite side from the one being limbed (so a glancing blow won't cut you) and try to remove each limb with one clean stroke. It'll take some power on stout limbs but the cleaner the cut, the easier the log will peel and the better the final appearance will be.

Once it's limbed, measure the tree carefully and mark it for log size. Cut the log longer than needed: There's nothing more frustrating than trying to use a log you've cut too short. Always stand uphill when bucking and use the wedge to prevent the bar from being pinched.

Finally, gather the limbs into a pile over the stump. It'll take a long time for the scars of your work to vanish from the forest, so clean up afterward. The limbs not only hide the stump, but provide a home for forest critters.

Because some sites are difficult to access, cabins can be pre-built elsewhere, dismantled, and trucked to the site for reassembly.

How long logs need to dry depends on the condition of the logs and the climate, as well as how they are stacked to dry. The logs above belong to Dick Quinn and have been stacked properly, as have these roof poles (right) stacked to dry on the rack next to Greg Birchard's cabin on the bank of the Yukon River at Eagle, Alaska.

Most cabins require 50 to 55 logs: 10 per wall, 5 for the ridgepole, purlins, and caplogs, and the remainder for the gables and sills. It's a lot of work harvesting that much timber. On a good day, cleaning up as I go, I cut 10 or 15 logs; it takes three to five days to harvest them all, depending on various factors like weather, terrain, and distance between suitable logs. I prefer to log in winter. It means extra work digging the snow away from the foot of the tree, but there are no bugs, heat, or brush to fight. And it does minimize the impact on the forest. Without fail, I always flag or mark with poles each and every log. An overnight snowfall can effectively hide downed timber until spring.

I can't emphasize enough that a major effort and/or expense will be getting the logs out of the woods and to the road or cabin site. Most four-wheel-drive pickups or cars won't handle large green logs, no matter what the salesman told you. Unless the logs are quite small or dead-standing, it takes heavy equipment, such as a tractor or tracked vehicle, or horses to do the job. It is possible to do your own logging and then hire out the hauling and trucking. A couple of folks on the Kenai Peninsula make a living doing just that.

In winter there's a cheap way to move logs out. On a good, packed trail, even a small recreational snow machine can move small to medium logs; some folks do it with a dog team. Other than the machine itself, all you need is a go-devil. A what? A go-devil—a small sled to support the front of the log. Supposedly the name comes from an Athabascan who pioneered using a sno-go to haul logs on the Yukon River winter trail. He hauled them tied to a shortened, home-built sled, and said they "go-like-devil." (Well, an Alaskan hunting guide told me this story, so it has to be true, doesn't it?) But it does work.

First, pack a trail from each log to the assembly point. Let the trail set up overnight. It's best to make the trail on a warm afternoon when the snow is soft, yet when it is still cold enough to freeze solid at night. March and April are the best months for this. Early the

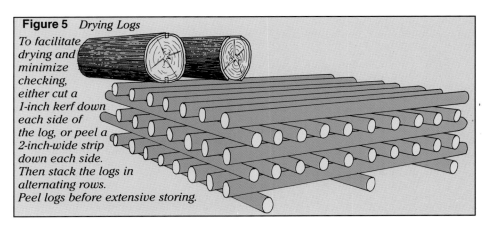

Figure 5 *Drying Logs*

To facilitate drying and minimize checking, either cut a 1-inch kerf down each side of the log, or peel a 2-inch-wide strip down each side. Then stack the logs in alternating rows. Peel logs before extensive storing.

next morning, well before the snow softens, start hauling. Face the machine in the right direction and put the butt end of the log up on the sled. Tie it down firmly. Sometimes, but not always, it's necessary to put something under the trailing end of the log; a plastic snow sled works well here. Make sure the log is fixed securely to the go-devil. Start the machine, stand next to it, give it the gas, shove if necessary, and, as the whole thing starts moving, jump on. Don't stop until you get to the final destination. Hopefully, the trail has no sharp turns and no uphills. This method works extremely well, although it might take a little experience designing the trail. On occasion, I've moved green logs so heavy it took two people to wrestle the end of a log up onto the go-devil. Sometimes the machine won't be able to start a big log, but with someone pushing at the moment the power is applied, it'll go. Almost any dead-standing log and small to medium-sized green log can be moved this way. This method doesn't scar the forest, either. However, if done incorrectly or incautiously—like hauling down icy inclines where the log could jacknife against the machine—the driver and/or snow machine could suffer trauma.

No matter the method, always haul the logs with the bark on. Although peeled logs dry out faster and are much lighter than unpeeled logs, hauling, loading, and unloading can ruin a log's appearance. Although some logsmiths disagree, green logs should be dried a

minimum of six months, and some more than a year. Dead-standing trees need to dry only as long as required by local climate, though they may need no drying time. Ideally, green logs can be cut in winter, peeled, stacked, and left to dry one summer and another winter. Of course, the ideal is not always possible.

For the best protection from weathering and checking, cover the log pile to prevent alternate wetting and drying, the cause of rotting and damage. Leave adequate ventilation from both ends of the pile.

I like to stack logs in one pile (see Figure 5 for proper stacking technique). Others like to sort the logs into two or four piles, one on either side of the foundation. However, I like to have them all in one spot, especially when using logs of varying size and quality, so I can compare and make appropriate choices.

To further minimize checking and to facilitate drying, score each log before stacking. This isn't necessary with very dry logs, but it is important with green logs. Peel a 2-inch-wide strip down each side of the log, exposing the wood fiber. Most of the drying cracks will appear along this scoring. Some logsmiths recommend cutting a groove down opposite sides of the log. While it is true that most of the cracking will localize to the kerf, the grooves will be difficult to hide and keep from showing on the wall. Chances are, parts of the kerf will show, so the scoring technique seems superior.

A cabin built with unpeeled logs has a certain crude charm and I suspect the

Big logs have many advantages: Fewer logs are needed to reach wall height, which means fewer notches have to be made (less work), and they have more insulative value, so the finished building is warmer. The walls of this home are only five logs high.

insects that inhabit the bark think so too. If you want your cabin to last, never leave *any* portion of the log unpeeled. Bark deteriorates unevenly, falls off inside and out, and allows moisture to accumulate and attack the wood fiber. Always peel it off.

Peeling logs can be hard work, but a good sharp drawknife can lessen the labor. Because of the sap content, green logs cut in the spring are the easiest to peel, while green, winter-cut logs, dried properly, are the hardest. (Though unseasoned logs are easy to peel, avoid building with them.) Some fire-killed logs can be very difficult to peel if the charring is deep. Dead-standing, beetle-killed logs can be easiest of all, with no bark at all to peel or with the bark falling off easily. Each log peels differently.

Most green logs and some fire-killed logs turn white or cream-colored when peeled. Peeled dead-standing timber looks russet and white, broken by the markings of the spruce bark beetle (*Dendroctonus rufipennis*). For best results, use either seasoned green-cut or dead logs, but not both, because of the color variations. Deep, uniform drawknifing can blend the two, but this effort is better applied elsewhere. Though not impossible, it's simply too difficult to match the color, texture, and appearance of the two types.

Whichever chosen, the rustic beauty of russet logs or the clear gold of fully peeled logs from live trees, each has its

own appeal. I like the color and markings of beetle-killed logs, but the brightness of white logs can help dispel the darkness of a small-windowed cabin.

The bark on green-cut logs should be peeled off uniformly. Both the outer and inner bark need to come off. The sappy inner layer, called the cambium layer, looks white when first exposed to the air, but turns brown when fully oxidized. For an all-white log, all of the inner bark must come off. I like to leave just a trace of the cambium layer here and there about the length of the log to add color. Others prefer to peel the log completely clean. By leaving some of the inner bark on green-cut logs and partially peeling through the brown wood on dead-cut, you can somewhat match the log types.

Fire-killed logs often require deep drawknifing to remove the charred areas, although underneath the wood is white and clean. An interesting effect can be achieved by leaving a slight charring here and there; the finished log will look as if it has been worked over with a child's wood-burning set. Most logs will have to be drawknifed or sanded down to uniform color and quality. Some builders peel the bark, then go over the whole log with a heavy-duty disc sander. Unless done judiciously, I think sanding leaves marks of an unpleasing appearance. I prefer to drawknife. Note: If you must sand, use only a heavy-duty *disc* sander, and always sand the logs

before putting them up. Sanding a finished cabin to remove weathering or marring is an unpleasant task unmatched by any other.

When peeling logs you'll be thankful you took the time to cut the limbs and knots off first. A knot cleanly removed with the ax adds to the beauty of a cabin log, whereas a gouge or knot stub not only looks unsightly but will catch and collect dirt and dust.

One last comment. In damp forest areas, peeled logs in the stack or on the building can mildew and mold. As the sap and moisture drain out of the wood, mildew can turn a beautiful white log an ugly all-black. I well remember the first cabin I built in the bush. The walls went up in warm, dry spring weather, and by the time I returned in late fall, those lovely logs had turned jet black. Despair. What to do? Back in town I bought four gallons of household bleach. Later that winter, I sloshed on a mixture of half water and half bleach, and the logs turned white. I then painted the whole building with the solution and it returned almost to its former color. Since then I've found that water and bleach will remove even the toughest and foulest mold and mildew, turning aged logs light. Oxalic acid crystals, sometimes sold as log bleach or barnacle remover—dissolved in water—will also do the job, but, unless very strong, this solution requires several applications. Bleach seems to be the best solution.

Paul McArthur is using a 14-inch drawknife to peel this log. Note that the log is on sawhorses and at a comfortable height to work on.

Once it was possible to go anywhere into unsettled lands, pick a spot, and build. No more. Homesteading, like cheap gasoline, died in the 1970s, although the State of Alaska does have limited Land Disposal Programs for residents; purchase price and quality vary.

Today in Alaska, with just the basic modern amenities—well or piped water and electricity—lands once considered unusable as homesites are being built on. The view takes on prime importance over formerly more critical factors. A change of perspective, though, seems in the works. Increasing numbers of people look apprehensively at the world and its energy shortages. Housing totally reliant on electricity for heat, cooking, and water seems more vulnerable than ever to the vagaries of weather and changing geopolitics. What happens when the power goes off? The winters turn extra cold? Fuel costs skyrocket? We've forgotten how to live with nature, too often living in spite of it. That cabin on the hill may have a glorious view of the bay, but in a pinch it's unlivable.

In one Southcentral Alaska community there's a $150,000 state-of-the-art log home located on choice river frontage. A dream home, yet it's all-electric. There is no wood stove, no propane cookstove, no emergency power of any kind. And when the power goes out, as happens in that windy, avalanche country, that family sits freezing in the dark. That's not my idea of a better way to live.

Site Selection and Planning

This is the view from the living room of the beautiful log home of Tom Klein and Anita Stelcel near Denali Park. Their home snugs back in the timber, a break from the constant winds that blow along the river.

Building the Alaska Log Home

How did the old-timers live? Some lived poorly, on the edge of survival. But others lived well and left behind a model for coping with nature. Going with the flow, not fighting it. Wandering through dense woods, I've stumbled on the rubble of many old cabins, cabins built in the densest, thickest timber. At first I believed they were built there to be close to logs and firewood. Although true, that's but part of the story.

In the North, the wind's a killer, drawing body heat away. Only insulation and proper nutrition (stoking the inner furnace) prevent exposure, or hypothermia. So, too, the wind draws the heat from a cabin. Heating a cabin exposed to a wind on a frigid arctic night requires stacks of firewood or gallons of expensive fuel. In the heavy timber, though, the wind breaks its back on the sheltering, insulating trees, and a cabin is more easily heated.

The wind can also drift snow into great heaps. For example, on Alaska's North Slope, a cold desert of very low annual snowfall, drifts as high as 16 feet form around the petroleum camp buildings, a result of near-constant winds off the treeless tundra. A cabin exposed to the wind can drift over or, if built on a lake or riverfront, be damaged by storm-tossed waves or crushed by ice heaves.

Invariably, near these old cabins I've found dependable, year-round water sources. Small creeks and springs seldom freeze solid, even in the coldest temperatures, and seem to have been the favored water source of northern hivernans.

Before making it sound as if the sourdoughs shared woods wisdom unknown today, an example of the opposite should be given. Overflow is a common cold-country phenomenon. With the advent of freezing temperatures, creeks, ponds, and rivers freeze over, yet the water underneath continues to flow. As the mercury plummets, the ice pushes down and thickens until the pressure intensifies enough to force the water up through cracks and onto the surface, eventually causing ice pans to widen dramatically and, in some cases, become several feet thick and hundreds of feet wide. Hidden and kept from freezing by a blanket of snow, the overflows run regardless of temperature and become a trap for the unwary. Overflow is a danger to cabins as well. One winter I saw an old hunter's cabin on the Wood River in the Alaska Range encased, inside and out, in overflow ice 2 feet thick. In summer one could not imagine that ice one-quarter mile wide and 3 feet thick could build up from a 6-inch-deep, foot-wide stream 50 yards away.

Natural shelter and proximity to building logs, firewood, and a dependable water supply are factors

This was my first bush cabin—a 16-foot-by-18-foot, two-sided-log trapper-style building. The low-pitched roof was chosen because of its heat retention, although judging from the heavy snow load, a steeper pitch might have been a better choice.

Site selection is very important and even a small rivulet can cause severe problems. Here, overflow is causing ice to build up the side of a two-sided-log cabin.

common to many old cabin sites. It would seem that the old-timers cared little about a view; protection from the elements was more important. Often their cabins were built with a blank, windowless wall facing some awesome panorama, with the few windows facing south, open to the warmth of the sun. Even today, southern exposure remains an important consideration when purchasing land.

The overflow in the Wood River cabin points out the importance of looking at the land in all seasons, not just in the summer. Good, year-round drainage is essential. What looks like solid, dry ground in midsummer may flood after spring or fall rains. Along rivers, creeks, or lakeshores, look for the natural signs of high water: flotsam tossed on the bank, or water-marked trees. Local residents can provide information about local conditions but they are not always accurate. An amazing amount of reliable climatic data for remote areas can be obtained from various government agencies. There's no such thing as a normal year, so check the snowfall and rain records, flood and drought histories. But don't go by statistics alone; see for yourself. It may be better to locate back away from the lake or river, foregoing the view in favor of security and privacy. Tucked away from the water, a cabin is less apt to be noticed by water travelers.

Ideally, build on solid, dry ground, with the foundation resting on rock or gravel. Dig down at the site and examine the soil. What's it like? Will it shift in heavy rain? Freeze solid in winter? How far down is bedrock or gravel? Remember, a log structure needs a great deal more support than a frame building of the same size.

In northern latitudes, depending on terrain features, soil type, moisture content, local climate, and insulative value of the ground cover, permafrost can pose problems for the cabin builder. (One definition of permafrost: soil that

remains frozen over a year.) Neither permanent nor continuous, permafrost can appear or disappear from an area. Clay, silt, or peat soils usually have high moisture and ice content. Avoid building on anything but coarse soils, gravel, or mixed types. These soils hold very little ice at freezing temperatures.

While it is possible to build on permafrost, using nonheat-conductive-type foundations or pads, avoid doing so. Even the best of foundations can shift unevenly on permafrost. The University of Alaska's Cooperative Extension Service can provide technical data for building on permafrost.

In mountain areas, avalanche danger can be extreme. Land below steep, open slopes should be avoided. Once I stayed in a frame cabin tucked away in an idyllic cove off Kachemak Bay. It was a beautiful spot, with open vistas of sea and forest, and fish to catch and bears to watch. Summertime and the slopes above stood free of snow and mantled in chest-high grass. The cabin, nestled in a grove of spruce, seemed safe, yet I wondered. In spring I'd seen thunderous avalanches roar down into bays like this one, sweeping all aside. That cabin remained the joy of the owner for five years. Now, a scarred, barren slope leads to the water's edge. Except for a few twisted and downed spruce, nothing remains of that copse and cabin.

Finally, what about access? Access by plane, boat, foot, or auto can be the

prime feature and main attraction of a land parcel. Some seek the solitude of a wilderness home, while others look for a drive-up, weekend retreat from the 9-to-5 world. Regardless, build for durability and practicality. Leave the trees to block the wind. Build slightly smaller than needed and save on fuel bills or cords of firewood. Consider all eventualities because much may depend on it. Where would you go if a forest fire raged through your area?

If and when a natural disaster should strike, or the world loses all its sanity, the cabin may prove to be a haven. Think about how the pioneers and settlers lived. Dig a root cellar, store a few staples. Have a wood stove, even if only an auxiliary. Keep emergency lighting handy, lanterns or oil lamps. And, finally, build a cabin compatible with the site and area selected.

The old, post-Russian, pioneer Alaska cabins looked surprisingly alike. Most were small, with few windows and low walls and low-pitched, sod-covered roofs. Most were built to retain heat, using only firewood, which was sometimes scarce. Unfortunately, most were built quickly and poorly; thus few functional ones survive.

Considering the numbers of cabins that had to have been built by the hordes of gold seekers that came north in the decades around the turn of the century, it's remarkable that so few

The home of Helen Rhode was built by her late husband, Cecil, on the shore of Kenai Lake. Note how many trees were left in front of the cabin to shield it from the winds. Some might have removed all the trees to improve the view, but that would not have been prudent from a practical standpoint. See also the photos on pages 137 and 154.

functional cabins remain from that era. The gold rush—a rush to get here, get rich, and get out—left no time to build anything to last. Where one day no sign of human activity marred the land, almost the next a city of thousands flourished. And, with the word of another strike, just as quickly vanished. In Europe, some log buildings have stood for 600 years, but in the New-World North, only relics and remnants remain.

Studying the best of the surviving cabins, or pawing through skeletal remains of the worst, I've found factors common to their demise or longevity. The foundation, notches, and roof prove to be the three critical factors in determining cabin life. In principle, each of these design features should protect the logs from moisture. Obviously, a roof that leaks, notches that let water stand, and a poor or nonexistent foundation that brings logs directly into contact with the soil will hasten cabin decay. Most of the sourdough cabins were built with one or more design faults.

The log corners in these early cabins fit in about as many ways as there were builders, with lapped, tenon, dovetail, saddle, and round notches most common, along with the trough, or plank,

corner. Some of this joinery contributed to the eventual decay of the logs by letting moisture accumulate and the wood rot. The best remaining sourdough cabins have logs joined with round notches. The round notch is a good, tight, weather-resistant notch.

Many of the early cabins were built directly on the ground, or at best supported with flat rocks. Logs just won't last used this way. A dead-standing tree actually does not begin to really decay until it falls and comes in contact with the moist soil; then it decays rapidly. Building directly on the ground hastens rot. Also, without a foundation, cabin heat melts the permafrost and the resulting thaw damages the structure.

A sod roof also spells an early demise for a cabin. A majority of the pioneer cabins had them because sod was the only available insulation and roofing material. Sod, though, holds moisture, which then seeps down to rot the roof boards, purlins, and ridgepole. Sod is also heavy and, coupled with a hefty snow load, puts a strain on and eventually weakens the roof supports. (An architect estimated that a sod roof for a 20-foot-by-24-foot cabin I built would weigh over 38,000 pounds!) All

Old sourdoughs used to build their cabins back in the heavy timber in order to be close to building logs and firewood, as well as to be protected from the wind. Moss and lichen are reclaiming this old doghouse found in heavy timber near the McKinley Bar. (E. A. Mills)

This log home on a bluff overlooking Kachemak Bay near Homer is shielded somewhat by the trees from the winds that are common to this area.

too many of the old cabins, otherwise well-built, collapsed from roof rot. A conventional roof, though perhaps not as authentic, protects a cabin far better than sod.

Admittedly, pole-and-sod roofs still go on cabins today and remain an inexpensive roofing and insulation. Dave Johnston, mountain climber and accomplished log builder, built a beautiful log sauna on the edge of a small pond near Denali. He put several layers of heavy plastic sheeting down over the poles as an effective moisture barrier. (Plastic is something the pioneers would have been grateful for.) He then covered that with scrounged carpeting and foam insulation scraps. Then came another sheet of plastic, followed by a thick covering of sod. Even on the coldest, subzero days, with the inside temperature a stove-roaring 170° F, or hotter, the roof supports a hefty snow load without any sign of heat loss. Best of all, a reflection of Dave's high wilderness ethic, the beetle-killed logs and sod roof blend naturally with the surroundings.

While each cabin design will vary, it will have features common to all other cabins. The individual requirements of the builder will show up in the plan. Obviously a 12-foot-by-14-foot cabin won't meet the needs of a family of six. Other factors, such as budget and intended use, will also affect the cabin plan. Once the costs of flooring, windows, doors, insulation, roofing, tools, gasoline and oil, and transportation are figured, it will be apparent that the price of logs, purchased or self-harvested, is not *the* major expense of the project.

As an example, throughout the book I detail the step-by-step construction of a 16-foot-by-18-foot trapper, or sourdough, cabin. The construction techniques described here will work for any size cabin or log home. I do not expect all builders to use my plan, nor do I offer alternate floor plans. Rather, this simple practical design serves as a good teaching example.

My first bush cabin was a 16-foot-by-18-foot trapper style, with the logs joined with round notches. It has three windows and one door, but needed a fourth and larger window. When we first moved to the bush from Interior Alaska, my prime concern, with a small infant to look after, was having a warm cabin. I didn't check local conditions as carefully as I should have, and the cabin turned out to be *too* warm, with the area's heavy snowfall adding insulation and the low roof becoming a liability that needed shoveling. The experience did prove the efficiency of the design, and I'd build another just like it in deep cold country, such as in the Tanana or Yukon River valley, or areas of low snowfall. Better to be too warm than cold.

The 16-foot-by-18-foot trapper cabin (Figure 6A), patterned after the best of the sourdough cabins but modified with a steeper-pitched roof, offers plenty of floor space for a minimal cash outlay. Another plan (Figure 6B), a variation of

the basic design, features an arctic entry. You might call this modification a passive-solar log cabin. Not a fancy, complex plan by any means, but an idea drafted directly from a 1920-era cabin on the banks of the Yukon River that's still in use today and is the easiest to heat and most comfortable cabin I've ever seen.

Even if you opt for a completely different design, the arctic entry remains an excellent idea. It helps keep the house warm, while at the same time providing extra storage space and a catch bin for tracked-in dirt and mud.

So how long would it take to build a *quality* 16-foot-by-18-foot cabin? Well, that's not easy to answer. Starting from scratch, with the logs peeled and ready to go, using the techniques outlined in this book, it'd take an expert a month or less. A novice, striving for fine craftsmanship, might take three times as

long. Give yourself plenty of time, and don't rush it. Of all the building skills, logwork especially falls prey to the basic law of the universe: Murphy's Law. "If anything can go wrong, it will." A number of factors, including, but not limited to, chainsaw breakdown, inclement weather, or injury (heaven forbid), can slow up or bring to stop a log project. This law especially applies to bush construction where the nearest ten-cent part is a $300 air charter away. Then, you can invoke O'Toole's Commentary on Murphy's Law: "Murphy was an optimist."

Critics have called the trapper design "functional rectangular," or worse, and lacking in creativity. Maybe so, but there's nothing like it for the novice to learn on. Later, once the basic log building skills are mastered, the only limiting factor becomes the logsmith's imagination.

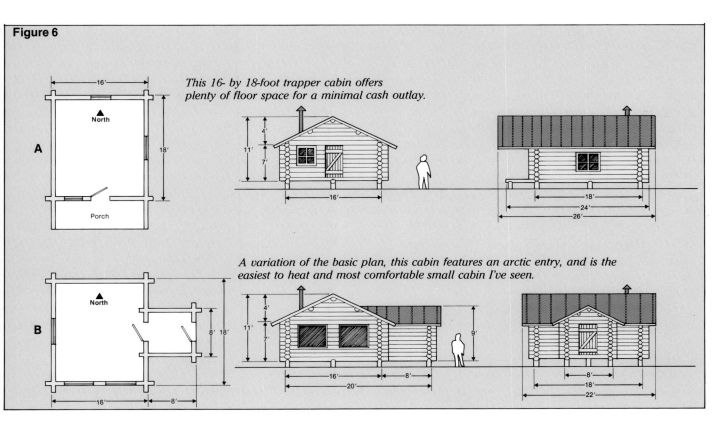

Figure 6

This 16- by 18-foot trapper cabin offers plenty of floor space for a minimal cash outlay.

A variation of the basic plan, this cabin features an arctic entry, and is the easiest to heat and most comfortable small cabin I've seen.

Whether the cabin brings pleasure for a lifetime or for only a few years depends largely on the quality of the foundation.

The main function of the foundation is to protect logs from rot. The foundation, then, should be left open, or built with ventilation openings to allow air circulation beneath the floor to minimize condensation and prevent rotting of sill logs and floor joists. Also, in cold country, a proper foundation is needed to prevent the harmful thaw of frozen ground.

The importance of careful site selection will be most apparent when excavating for the foundation. Many poorly chosen sites have been abandoned when excavations filled with water or ooze, turning the holes into little mosquito ponds.

The strongest, longest-lasting foundation, offering the best weight distribution, is a continuous wall of block or poured concrete over a standard footing. In remote or rural areas, or when budget prohibits, other types of foundations work well on small or medium-sized cabins. Since concrete or block foundations are common to more conventional construction projects, I'll focus instead on alternate and more economical types suited to rural or inaccessible sites.

Commonly, cabins are built on wood posts or pilings, an inexpensive favorite of bush Alaskans. Old telephone poles or wharf pilings work best and last longest because of creosote pressure-treating. Untreated wooden posts in contact with soil do not last long before rot sets in. Treated wood, called "green-wood," pilings are available from commercial suppliers and are meant for direct placement on soil. A house is only

as good as the foundation. A few builders envelop the below-ground portion of dry posts in plastic bags or sheeting for moisture-proofing.

Posts should be a minimum diameter of 10 inches and extend above ground no less than 18 inches. Post holes should be dug to a depth below frost line and the posts should rest on firm, compacted soil. They should be placed at corners and intervals of 8 to 10 feet. (Never use short-life woods, such as birch and aspen, for posts.) Level the tops with one another using a level-transit or a string level and line.

Concrete piers, which are more permanent than posts, can be easily constructed at rural or remote sites. Piers should also be placed at corners and at 8- to 10-foot intervals under walls, and extend below the frost line. You can make forms of scrap boards or plywood at the site and mix the concrete by hand. (Always use clean sand or the mix won't set up properly.) Piers should be leveled before pouring and be at least 8 inches square.

Some soils, due to moisture content, composition, and permafrost, become unstable when disturbed. The least disturbance—and the avoidance of heat transference—the better. In some areas, piers and posts are preferred over continuous foundations. I saw one bush cabin, built on permafrost, that sat on concrete piers that had been made from gasoline-can forms. Another cabin in a swampy area was built on 55-gallon drums buried in the wet soil and filled with rocks. Commercial cardboard forms, called Sonatubes, are most commonly used. Steel reinforcing rods, called rebar, should be inserted in the forms for strength and for attachment of stringers.

Another simple form can be made using 30-pound tarred felt (tar paper). Make a cylinder of two thicknesses of felt the desired diameter, say 10 inches. Starting at one end and working toward the other, wrap cord around the roll to hold it together, or staple it to a lath. This form, then, will measure 10 by 36 inches. Stand the cylinder in the hole and backfill lightly around the base just enough to support it and level the top to proper height. Next, carefully pour a few inches of concrete into the form. Backfill around it to that level. Then pour in more

Foundations

The Peanut Farm Lounge in Anchorage on the bank of Campbell Creek is a good example of Lee A. Cole's work—one of Alaska's master logsmiths. Cole's first public building in Alaska was the Anchorage Visitors Center; see page 158.

Sill log bolted to the platform. The top of the bolt will be cut off before the next log goes on the wall. The tar is to keep the water out during construction.

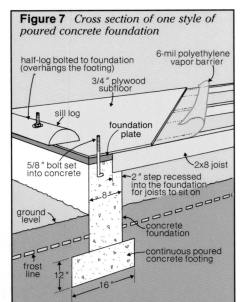

Figure 7 *Cross section of one style of poured concrete foundation*

half-log bolted to foundation (overhangs the footing)

6-mil polyethylene vapor barrier

3/4" plywood subfloor

sill log

foundation plate

5/8" bolt set into concrete

2x8 joist

2" step recessed into the foundation for joists to sit on

8"

ground level

concrete foundation

frost line

continuous poured concrete footing

12"

16"

Many types of foundations support log buildings. The size and shape of a concrete footing depends largely on soil conditions; soft or damp soils require a wide footing so that there is no possibility of settlement. Standard footings are usually twice as wide as the foundation wall and as thick as the wall width. Because foundations under a log building support a heavy, concentrated load, the footing should be thicker than standard. Our sample shows a footing one and a half times as thick as the foundation wall is wide. (Check local building codes, if any.) The poured concrete example features a step, or recess, on the inner portion of the footing for the joists to sit on. The plywood subflooring will extend out over the concrete. A half-log is then bolted to the building with the aid of prepositioned bolts set into the concrete; the bolts vary in spacing, but on an 18-foot wall, four would be sufficient. Note that the footing in this soil extends below the frost line.

concrete and backfill some more. Alternately pour and backfill as you work up to ground level; the soil will support the form. The portion of the felt above ground can also be supported with dirt, or may possibly support the concrete by itself. The felt also provides a good moisture seal for the pier.

In Southeast Alaska I once saw a cabin foundation built of local rock and mortar, a true marvel. The 10-inch-thick foundation, footed on solid rock, climbed 8 feet upward in front, while the back portion of the rockwork, also poured on rock, rose only 12 inches; the side walls sloped over the irregular rock land surface to the sea-facing front wall. The rock, sand, concrete, rebar—all the materials, for that matter—were hauled in a dory from a larger bay a mile distant. Barring an earthquake, a 200-foot tsunami, or a nuclear holocaust, that foundation will stand the test of time.

Once you have chosen a suitable foundation, clear the actual cabin site, removing only the undergrowth and trees directly in the work area. Level the ground as much as is practical. Using a long tape, mark off the cabin dimensions as closely as possible, trying hard to keep the sides parallel and square. (To be square, the corners must have right angles or, instead of being a rectangle, your building will be a parallelogram.) Mark the corners with stakes and run taut string lines between them to indicate wall lines.

The importance of having a perfectly squared foundation cannot be overemphasized. If the foundation isn't laid out correctly, the entire project will suffer. In the absence of a transit, the accuracy of the corner right angles can be checked with the 6-8-10 method. A triangle with sides of 6, 8, and 10 feet is an exact right triangle (Figure 8). Measure and mark off distances of 6 and 8 feet on the string lines. Then measure the diagonal line (hypotenuse) of the triangle, which, if a right angle, will be 10 feet. If it is not, then the angle is not a right angle. Check all four corners with this method and adjust the stakes as necessary. As a final check, measure diagonally from

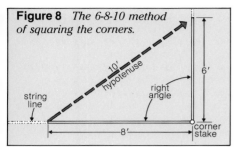

Figure 8 *The 6-8-10 method of squaring the corners.*

one corner of the cabin to the other. If the two diagonal measurements are the same, the layout is square.

A more permanent method of indicating the layout uses batter boards (Figure 9). Batter boards, right angles of boards nailed to stakes, are set up 4 feet outside the actual cabin layout. String lines, corresponding to the squared layout staked to the ground, are strung between the batter boards and, after measuring and checking their square, a nail or notch marks the spot on the boards where the lines fasten. Using the nails or notches as guides, the lines can then be taken down when not needed and replaced in the correct spot without further remeasuring. Use the boards with any style foundation.

With the foundation in, it's time to frame the floor. In modern frame construction, the floor is built over the foundation like a platform. On concrete foundations, for example, sills are bolted directly to the foundation. Joists, on 16-inch centers, span the building and are nailed to headers resting on the sills. Then the plywood or board flooring is nailed down. Called platform framing, this method provides a base upon which carpenters can assemble wall sections and raise them into place. This is a very stable and safe working surface, which is especially important for log builders using carnivorous chainsaws.

Many professional logsmiths work over a floor built much this same way, the only variation being that many prefer more substantial headers than, say, the usual 2x material. Usually, the first round of logs is set on the platform and attached to the foundation through the flooring.

The first round of logs is attached to the foundation with bolts or rebar.

Logsmith Dick Quinn bolts the initial round to the foundation. Other logsmiths, claiming that no bolting is necessary, simply drill the first round and place the logs down over rebar sticking up from underneath.

In Interior Alaska, one log builder begins by bolting 10x10 timbers to the top of the foundation (concrete, block, post, or pier). Then he attaches the joists to the timbers with metal hangers. The plywood subflooring goes on next and he's ready to start the logwork. He begins with a half-log for the end logs, standard for most logsmiths, and fits and notches the first round into place. Finally he drills at intervals down through the logs into the 10x10s. Then he drives in rebar, attaching the logs to the foundation. The walls proceed upward from that start.

Logsmiths vary greatly in their methods, quite noticeably in how they do post and pier foundations and floors. Some claim that the first logs must be attached directly to the foundation, or roll might occur. Others say the logs need only sit on the platform, claiming the logs aren't going to move, except in a major earthquake. Logsmiths are individuals and there seems to be no right way agreeable to all.

Personally, I like to bolt timbers to the posts or concrete, hang the joists from them, put on the plywood, and begin. (One builder I know grooves the tops of posts and stands a beam on edge in the slots. He then nails the joists to this header.) I then attach my half-logs to the platform and through the foundation with prepositioned bolts or rebar. Note: The end logs are halved so that the wall logs fit over them notched half their thickness, thus beginning the entire joinery process. If you want log sills and joists, here's an alternate way to proceed.

Pick out three straight, equal-size logs (base logs) for the sills. (Small cabins, say up to 12 feet by 14 feet, need not have a center log.) On a 16-by-18-foot cabin, sills should be 24 feet long or longer, allowing for rear projection and a 4-foot or greater front projection for porch support (Figure 10). Face the butts of all three sill logs toward the front. Flatten bearing surfaces where the logs rest on posts or piers, or their entire length if using a continuous foundation.

When using posts to support three base logs, it is best not to support the middle of the center log with a post. The posts supporting the walls bear a

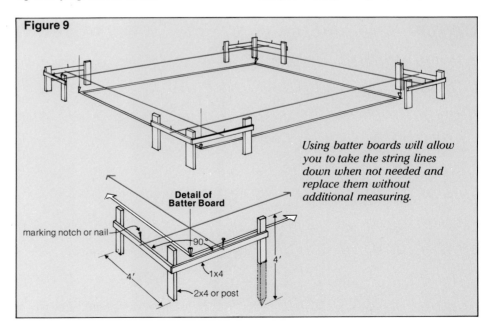

Figure 9

Using batter boards will allow you to take the string lines down when not needed and replace them without additional measuring.

Detail of Batter Board

marking notch or nail

1x4

2x4 or post

tremendous load and will settle differently from posts supporting the interior sections of a middle base log. The center should be supported only by blocks and be wedged at the top. As the cabin settles, the middle sill may tend to bow up, or crown, at the central support points. You can remove the wedges and blocks as needed to keep your floor level.

Next pick out two end logs, 20-footers on a 16-foot-by-18-foot cabin. The first end logs should be of large diameter. Using the method described in the following chapter, the end logs should be round-notched *half* their thickness and fit over the sill logs. Carefully check the square of the logs using the 6-8-10 and diagonal methods; adjust as necessary. This placement forms the shape of the cabin and should be done with care and accuracy. Finally, drill and

peg the end logs where they cross the sills. (I use the term "end logs" to indicate the short span of logs; wall logs refer to the long spans.)

Now the floor joists go in: hewn-log or milled lumber. Log joists should be 6 inches in diameter for 12-foot spans, 8 inches in diameter for 16-foot spans, and 10 inches for 20-foot spans. For dimensional-lumber joists, use 2x8s for 12-foot spans, 2x10s for 16-foot spans, and 2x12s for 20-foot spans. With logs or boards, place the joists on 16-inch centers. (If you are using milled lumber for joists and you begin this way, simply nail or bolt headers to the sill logs and hang the joists with metal hangers.)

Log joists are best fit with a gain and tenon (Figure 11), but also can be notched into place. (Some logsmiths point out that a tenon weakens the joist

at a stress point.) Before cutting the tenon, hew the joist logs flat on top. One way is to flatten the top side with an ax or adz. For the novice this may not be as easy as it sounds. It is very important to have a level surface so that the floor boards or plywood will lie flat. A chainsaw with a mill attachment will do a more accurate job.

The gain (slot) can be cut with a chisel, and the tenon (tongue) with a chisel and a handsaw. Make the fit as tight as possible. Before drilling and pegging the joists to the sills, make sure they are all level.

The floor boards and insulation can go in now or later. It may be a good idea to wait until the roof is on and most of the heavy work completed so that the floor materials are not damaged by rain, construction methods, or falling logs.

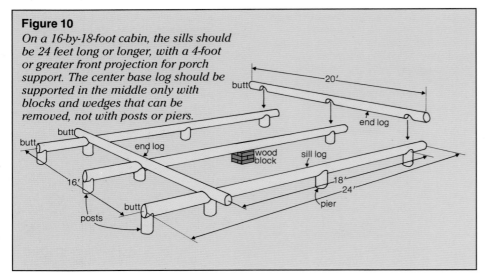

Figure 10

On a 16-by-18-foot cabin, the sills should be 24 feet long or longer, with a 4-foot or greater front projection for porch support. The center base log should be supported in the middle only with blocks and wedges that can be removed, not with posts or piers.

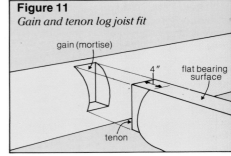

Figure 11

Gain and tenon log joist fit

Log floor joists in a building in Talkeetna, Alaska. Logwork by Steve Cross.

Log builder Harry Aulman's home in Talkeetna sits on a block basement. Note the careful scribe-fitting of the logs, the frame gables, and the way the log ends protrude outward to support the roof overhang. Aulman is a graduate of the B. Allan Mackie School of Log Building in British Columbia.

Pat Reinhardt and Greg Mantell-Hekathorn built this cabin for Louise Woods in Kobuk. The cabin is built on spruce posts; note the extra cross-bracing at the corners. (Ole Wik)

Logsmith Monroe Robinson used stone supports for this addition on a guest cabin at Jay Hammond's place at Lake Clark. (Monroe Robinson)

ogs have been joined in many ways with notches of all kinds. The common types of notches used include the round, saddle, dovetail, tenon, lapped, and V-notch. There is another notch, however, which I call the "Oh-my-gosh! What-is-it?" notch. This notch, which might be the most ubiquitous of all Alaskan notches, is formed by wildly hacking away at the log ends with ax or chainsaw or unidentifiable tools until the logs fit somewhat together. This notch is always used in conjunction with unpeeled logs, with the gaps between the logs chinked with saplings as big as the logs themselves. I hope the "Oh-my-gosh! What-is-it?" notch will soon disappear forever from the Alaska scene.

Figure 12 illustrates the most common notches.

Round Notch—Chapter Six details the unique qualities of the round notch and describes how to make it. In summation, the round notch is the best all-around notch for log joinery because of its strength and weather-resistancy. Also, it is not a difficult notch to learn to make, and the skill to make it is easily acquired.

Saddle Notch—Although a round notch is sometimes called a saddle notch, the two are actually quite different. The saddle notch is a Lincoln Log style, with cuts made in both the top and bottom of a log. Either cut square or, more uncommonly, rounded, the saddle notch can be shaped with a chainsaw or ax, and stoutly locks logs together. Still in favor in Appalachia and the South, this style of log joinery came

The Gakona Roadhouse was built in 1905 on the Richardson Highway and was originally called Doyle's Ranch. In 1919 the Trading Post or General Store was added on. The building is 21 rounds high and, unlike most buildings of the era, the walls are plumb. The logs were fit with square notches.

north with turn-of-the-century gold seekers. Of all the notch styles, however, this one is the least weather- and moisture-resistant. Water is freely admitted and soaks into the cut made in the top part of the log, resulting in quick decay. Of all the cabins I've studied, those built with saddle notches displayed the worst decay and rot damage.

Dovetail Notch—Russians and Scandinavians used the dovetail notch to lock squared logs together, but it also may be used to fit round logs. It takes quite a bit of practice and experience to make precision dovetail notches, and the resulting product may not be worth the effort. Although strongest of all

Log Joinery

These round notches and two-sided logs were crafted by Paul Smith of Cooper Landing, a master of two-sided-log construction.

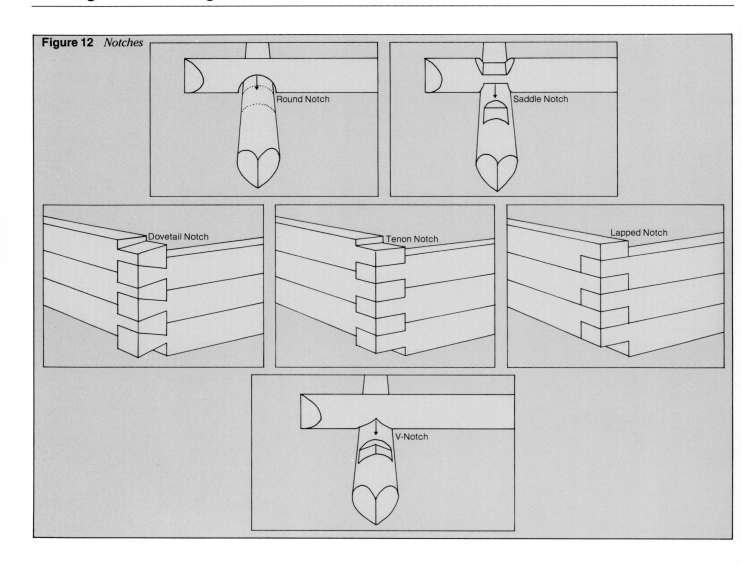

Figure 12 *Notches*

Round Notch

Saddle Notch

Dovetail Notch

Tenon Notch

Lapped Notch

V-Notch

The square notches and gaps between logs on this 1930s-era cabin on the Tanana River are chinked with mud.

interlocking notches, dovetails collect moisture and rot out quite readily. Many dovetail-notched, hewn-log structures are eventually covered with siding to protect the walls from the weather.

Tenon Notch—Commonly a tenon (tongue) is cut into the ends of the log and laps over the tenons of intersecting logs. The main difference between this notch and the dovetail is that the unbeveled tenon merely sits on the next log, rather than locks logs together. The tenon is a very simple notch to make but it is quite weak and has the same susceptibility to water damage as the saddle notch. An uncommon variation of the tenon notch, used with squared logs or timbers, fits the tenon into a mortise, or slot, cut into the end of the intersecting log. Each log has a tenon cut in one end and a mortise in the other. Then the logs are stacked, tenons fitting into mortises to form the corners. The major drawback here is that although each log of the round interlocks, the rounds themselves do not. The logs are merely stacked one on another and must be spiked together. The tenon and mortise notch is not weather resistant.

Lapped Notch—A multitude of variations of this notch exist, but most commonly the downside half of a log end is cut square and lapped over a similarly shaped intersecting log. Other than speed and simplicity, this notch has little to recommend it. It is structurally weak, lets water accumulate, and, unless chinked and rechinked regularly, results in drafty corners. Because it lends itself to dimensional construction techniques, the lapped notch finds favor with some timber and squared-log builders.

V-Notch—This is a variation of the saddle notch, in which a large V-cut is made in the top and bottom of the log. The V-notch is a simple interlocking device, prone to weather-induced decay. A good V-notch is time-consuming and somewhat difficult to make. Consequently, horrible examples of

Father Targonsky examines the logwork exposed during the 1979 restoration of Holy Assumption of the Virgin Mary Russian Orthodox Church in Kenai. The church was built in 1895 and is covered inside and out with siding, so the logs are not usually visible (see page 159). Note the dovetail notches, star, and moss chinking. (Mary Ford)

This very unusual lock notch, sometimes called a lapped lock notch, is believed to be of Finnish or Russian origin. The building, near Kasilof on the Kenai Peninsula, is believed to date from about 1900 and is the only structure I have seen in Alaska with all the corner notches constructed in this manner. (Mary Ford)

Recycled logs: John Hewitt of Fairbanks
is building this V-plank-corner outhouse
with logs salvaged from an old outhouse;
the logs were first cut in 1953. The new
facility is a three-holer. Drawknifing
revealed the white wood underneath.

I built this cabin at Loon Lake with
vertical log corners. The corners were
flattened on two sides and then
chinked with moss. The main drawback
to this design is that the logs do not
settle properly.

crude V-notches abound. Both the saddle notch and V-notch are the hurry-up, get-it-done-regardless-of-quality choices for log construction. These types are most common in 1950-vintage homesteads or hunting camps.

Many of these notches are best suited to round logs, although some may be used with any log style, including squared timbers. Some hastily built cabins have no notches. Instead, the logs were merely butted together, overlapped, or otherwise stacked together in a square or rectangular cabin shape. Usually some chinking—mud, plaster, or moss—filled the gaps between the logs. Sometimes, however, large gaps are purposely left between the logs to be chinked later with plaster or mud. This method is called the Colorado-style.

V-Plank Corner—Also called the Hudson Bay, trough, plank, Maine plank, or quick corners, this style of joinery is very common throughout Alaska and Yukon Territory. In this style, two boards, cut to desired wall height, are nailed together and fastened upright to the foundation at each of the four corners. Then logs are cut to length, fit between the corner uprights, and spiked to the planks as well as to each other. Commonly, the logs are not hewn, but left whole. Chinking, held in place with poles, fills the gaps. Generally, the corners are framed over on the outside, or a quarter-round log is set upright in the V. Some builders use quarter-round logs instead of planks at the corners, with the logs toenailed to the uprights. V-plank corners are aptly called quick corners since two men working together might easily build the walls on a small cabin in one day.

Plank corners can and have been used with both peeled and unpeeled logs, as well as with two-sided and scribe-fit logs, although since the logs are nailed to the planks and fixed in place, they'll shrink apart instead of properly settling together. Over time, most cabins built with plank corners show the inherent structural weakness of the design: Either huge gaps appear between the logs and constantly need rethinking, or the walls bow outward as the roof, under a snow load, exerts

Square tenon notches on a cabin in Talkeetna.

Wendell Hobbs of Fairbanks and a bar notch. The bar notch allows you to leave extra wood in the notch area to strengthen the notch when you would otherwise have to remove too much wood to allow the log to fit over the one below. Note that the notch is well over half the thickness of the log.

This photo dramatically illustrates the inherent weakness of V-plank corners.

Building the Alaska Log Home

Jack and Diana Greene's home in Eagle is built of two-sided 8-inch logs obtained from Arctic Inland Resources in Dawson City, Yukon Territory. The logs are joined at the corner with a blind, semi-dovetail notch of Jack's own ingenuity. For another view of the Greenes' home, see page 152.

The Klukwan Tribal House site near Haines has lapped corners. Klukwan is the headquarters for the Chilkat tribe, a branch of the Tlingits known for the blankets they weave from the long hair of mountain goats and cedar bark fibers.

Lapped corners on Lewis Reith's cabin in Moose Pass. The cabin was built 45 or 55 years ago by Ray Stafford and several others; the chinking is plaster.

Dave Johnston built this vertical, or stockade-style, log sauna of dead-standing timber on the edge of a small pond. Users can heat it up, then plunge through a hole cut in the ice to cool off. I found it refreshing! Dave built a special door so wood could be loaded directly into the barrel stove, and used aluminum sheets to cover the wood around the stove and on the door.

Vertical log construction is not always fast, however. The Leland Brewer family of Seward cut all their logs, prepared them, and did all the work themselves— it took three years from the time the first log was cut until they moved in. Of course, they weren't working continuously.

Dick Dickman of Seward cutting rough-cut lumber at his mill Construction with milled logs is usually cheaper (when hiring out the labor) and faster than with whole logs.

outward pressure and causes the planks to part. Eventually, structural failure at the corners causes collapse.

Stockade Logs — In this style, short sections are fit together in a vertical format, instead of being used horizontally. Starting from a platform or up from a sill log, log sections are stood on end and spiked together. First, a log framework is fashioned. Uprights are placed at each corner, with plate logs tying them together. Then, starting at a corner and working around the building, log sections fill the gap from the sills to the plate log and are spiked at the bottom to the adjoining log or to the sill log and the plate log. Many times the logs are whole and unhewn, the gaps between filled with chinking or plaster. Other times, a chainsaw is run up and down between the uprights until a close fit is achieved. Some builders use a stockade-style format to fill in gaps beneath windows, or to otherwise break up the basic horizontal look of a log cabin.

This style especially appeals to those working alone and without power equipment, as logs are short, manageable, and easily loaded on a sled; short sections are more readily peeled than full-length logs; and, except for raising the plate logs, one person can fit and install all the wall sections without any extra manpower or mechanical aid.

Despite these advantages, however, stockade logs never settle but, rather, shrink apart, opening gaps and undoing all the work that went into fitting them together. On a cabin built entirely stockade-style, you might be able to live with this problem, since it is to be accepted as an integral part of the design. However, vertical sections, even if only used around windows and doors, should be avoided on cabins built primarily of horizontal logs. The vertical logs, with their inability to settle, will cause problems galore with the adjoining horizontal logs. Most usually, gaps will form between the horizontal logs, or sections will bow and settle differently from those supported by the uprights. Too, as the horizontal logs settle, they'll exert force on vertical sections that may cause structural

failure. Vertical log walls should never be used to build a large cabin, but if used, central tie logs are a must.

Two-sided Logs — In the early part of Alaskan history, a major technological development occurred with the arrival to a settlement of a sawmill. The mill turned logs into boards, enabling construction to proceed faster and more cheaply. Those still wanting to build with logs then had the option of using whole logs or having two sides of a log slabbed flat. Usually these two-sided logs were butted together or lapped at the corners, but were seldom notched. Today, two-sided logs from mill stocks are not only slabbed flat on two sides but are often power-peeled. Milled two-sided logs offer a uniformity that home-milled logs can't match. However, the builder who mills his own logs can minimize waste, using every fraction of an inch of log thickness, all without milling marks to sand off.

Three-sided Logs — Russians and Scandinavians used broadaxes and saws to slab-flat the inside and outside faces of their logs, a minimum waste of 25% of the wood fiber and insulative value of the log. Some Alaskan pioneers used logs in a similar way. I've seen many cabins, most dating from the 1920s or earlier, with inside, outside, and bearing surfaces broadaxed flat.

Siding logs this way is time-consuming and labor-intensive work. Probably as a response, the three-sided log, as well as other types, came into existence. A mill slabs three sides of a log flat, creating a uniform 6- or 8-inch thickness, and leaves the fourth side round and unpeeled. Three-sided logs are very popular, quite probably the most common log-like building material in use today, partly because they're widely available, and partly because three-sided logs are very easy to work with. A three-sided-log house goes up quite quickly since the logs need only be peeled on one side, and then usually butted or lapped together, rather than notched. Three-sided logs give the first-timer experience working with large, heavy materials; even an inexperienced builder can put up a relatively nice three-sided-log cabin as a first attempt.

Two-sided logs fitted, not notched, together by Paul Yarbrough.

A three-sided-log cabin near Homer. Most three-sided logs are "butt and run construction, with no notches at the corners. Three-sided logs are a good training medium for gaining experience in dealing with nonconventional building materials. The roofing is aluminum.

Three-sided logs are popular not only because of availability and ease of construction but because of the more conventional appearance and versatility of interior wall surfaces. A cabin built of three-sided logs from the outside looks much like a real log cabin, but on the inside has flat, straight walls. For the most comfortable living space, inside log surfaces should be sanded since sawmarks are quite prominent and collect dirt and snag clothing.

Most sawmills offer three-sided logs in 6- and 8-inch sizes. The vertical dimension, 6 or 8 inches, remains constant, but the horizontal measurement may vary because the exterior round portion of each log is quite irregular. In most of Alaska, an 8-inch log should be considered minimum size for residential use. Even a good 6-inch log, with little horizontal variation in thickness, does not have enough insulative value to be a practical choice for northern climatic conditions. Unfortunately, some mills can produce only a limited amount of 8-inch logs due to the poor quality or size of local timber, and 6-inch three-sided logs may be the only size available. However, know at the outset that it might be necessary to fur out and insulate the inside walls to gain any degree of heat retention and efficiency with three-sided 6-inch or even 8-inch logs. With this in mind, you might be better off opting for a different log style, or perhaps choosing one of the latest superinsulated frame house designs.

In terms of simplicity of assembly and speed, no other log style compares to three-sided-log construction. Yet even with three-sided logs, you must cope with settling. If put together properly, that is, allowing for appropriate settling space above doors, windows, and partitions and spiking the logs only

through drilled holes, three-sided logs can settle together more tightly than most any other log style. Usually, though, the corners aren't tight enough to prevent air infiltration and heat loss. For best results, it's generally wise to caulk the exterior gaps between three-sided logs.

Three-sided logs of any dimension are not cheap. A few years ago, squared 10x10 spruce timbers from a Fairbanks mill cost considerably less than 8-inch three-sided logs. One log builder took advantage of the situation and bought the 10x10s, drawknifed the edges, axed the inside and outside surfaces to mimic broadax markings, and fit the timbers together with square notches. The resulting log house looked for all the world to be hand-hewn squared timbers, and proved warmer than any 8-inch three-sided-log house could ever be.

Another logsmith, Jimmy Hitchcock of Caribou Cabin Company in Wasilla, specializes in custom three-sided-log construction. There are some 150 Hitchcock-built homes spread all over Alaska from Fairbanks to Girdwood, trademarked by 8-inch-by-12-inch open truss beams and interlocking notched corners. Hitchcock has been building log cabins in Alaska since 1957.

The demand for log cabins and structures exceeds supply. Until the recent renaissance of the art of log building, logsmiths were few and far between, and the good ones could not keep pace. Consequently, prefabricated log kits came into being.

Turned Logs—Many sawmills sell turned, or milled, logs, either tapered or of uniform diameter. Whole logs are put on a lathe, which limits the available length of such logs, and turned to size. Tapered logs are slabbed on two sides and machine-notched at both ends. Turned logs of uniform size, either 6-, 8-,

or 10-inch diameters, are also available with prefabricated notches. Some are milled flat on two sides, but most are turned with a concave lateral groove in scribe-fit style.

Turned logs can be purchased piecemeal, or as a kit complete with assembly instructions. They are quite easy to work with but have several limitations. In my opinion, unless all the milling marks are sanded off, turned logs have an unpleasant finished appearance. Lathe cutters leave unsightly gouges and the log ends are marred by holes where they were attached to the lathe. The major drawback, however, is that since only relatively short sections of turned logs are available, the logs must be spliced together if the planned structure is to be of any size.

Kits of all kinds, mostly milled or turned logs, are available from sawmills or large manufacturers. (I'm not referring here to cedar timber homes, such as Pan-Abode, Scandia, or Justus Homes. These are timber conceptions, and not log.) Aimed at the do-it-yourselfer, these kits, labeled anything from "genuine log cabins" to "authentic log homes," aren't any of these. Rather, most are processed, standardized log-like home packages, although there are exceptions. Not all prefabricated log homes should be snubbed. Some builders, using natural logs and round-notch, scribe-fit techniques, offer units for reassembly elsewhere. Logsmith Jimmy Hitchcock of Palmer builds log homes for relocation. His are quality, handcrafted log homes built of native spruce logs.

Generally speaking, however, in terms of uniqueness and quality, carbon-copy, turned-log kits come out second best when compared to quality-built, natural log structures.

Milled-log cabin on the shore of Beluga Lake, Homer. Wall lengths are pieced together.

This new milled-log home for Julie Waugh in Eagle replaces the burned cabin owned by her late husband, master guide Hal Waugh.

Nice round notch on a scribe-fit log.

Your finished cabin will be judged on many features, not least of which will be the corner notches. Logsmiths usually look first at the notches when measuring craftsmanship. Also, this is the one detail that most impresses the novice or casual admirer. In short, the quality of the notches, both in aesthetics and function, will make or break the project.

A good notch not only joins logs together but also seals in heat and, more important, keeps out moisture. All manner of notches have joined logs, but only the round notch offers a combination of features. True, some types of notches may lock logs together better, but they turn up short in other regards, especially in resisting moisture.

In many areas, round notches are called saddle notches, but actually the two are quite different. (Don't be confused by terminology: Just remember an actual saddle notch looks like those on Lincoln Logs.) The saddle notch is made by cutting into both the upper and lower sides of a log, whereas to make a round notch, only the down or under side of a log is cut. Thus, water runs off of and not into the notch, thereby preventing rot and extending the life of the cabin.

Ideally, the round notch should follow precisely the curvature of the lower log without so much as a knife blade's gap between the two. The notch should also remain tight and not open up as the logs shrink and the cabin settles. A good notch should fit as tightly 10 years after construction as the day it was made. In fact, an expertly made round notch may fit even *tighter* with time. This may sound impossible, but it's not. Expertly

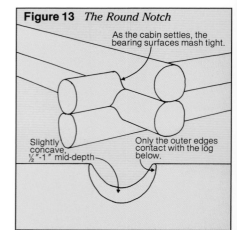

Figure 13 *The Round Notch*

As the cabin settles, the bearing surfaces mash tight.

Slightly concave, ½"-1" mid-depth

Only the outer edges contact with the log below.

A proper round notch is slightly concave, resembling a bowl. If scribed and cut out accurately, the notch will not need external sealants. The hollow can be filled with insulation that will not show. Of all the various types of notches, the round notch probably offers the best combination of features: it seals the heat in, locks the logs together, and keeps the moisture out — rain runs off instead of into the notch.

The Round Notch

Tom Klein of McKinley cutting a notch—
note the pencil line below the chain bar.

A tight notch depends on the accuracy of the scribe markings. The best investment a builder can make is in a quality scribe with level attachment.

A notch ready to be cut out. Normally only a thin pencil line indicates the area to be notched, but this line was darkened for the photograph. Strive for a neat, thin pencil line and never cut away all the line; rather, cut through the middle of it.

done, a round notch will be somewhat concave, or cupped, with only a thin outer edge touching the log below. As the building settles and the weight pushes down, this thin bearing surface will mash flat and the notch will tighten instead of opening up. A notch so constructed (Figure 13) can be filled with loose insulation that won't show, and will be tight enough not to need any tar, sealant, caulk, or other gunk applied to the outside surface.

There's really no secret; anyone—yes anyone—can do expert notching; you just need a scribe and patience to do the work right.

Before beginning the actual cabin project, make a few practice notches. Take short sections of peeled logs and experiment. See what works best for you, and what doesn't. Get an idea of what the chainsaw can and can't do. (It can't cut round lines.) Find out how well the hand tools cut various woods. Practice and try for a good, tight notch. Take your time and learn the right way to do it.

Begin with two log sections of the same diameter. Block them up so that one crosses the other at a right angle, as would be the case at an actual log corner. Level both logs. Open the scribe (wing dividers) to half the diameter of the logs where they cross. For example, a 10-inch-thick log will require a 5-inch-deep notch and scribe setting. Now, holding the scribe vertical and level (watch the bubbles, not the pencil), trace the curvature of the bottom log, keeping the upper wing point (pencil point) in firm contact with the crossing log. Repeat the process on the reverse side of the log. If the scribe has been kept level, the mark on the upper log will correspond exactly to the shape of the lower log (Figure 14).

Most professionals use an indelible pencil (ink pencil) in the upper wing of the scribe. The ink pencil will leave a mark even on wet wood and is ideal for scribing and making notches. Some builders darken the pencil line with crayon or marker, but if you do, make sure the secondary marking follows the scribe line exactly and does not vary from it. A good tight fit depends on the exactness of the scribe line. For

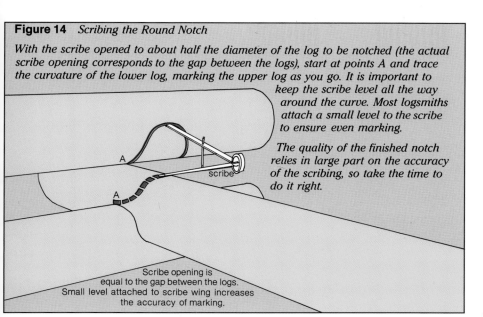

Figure 14 *Scribing the Round Notch*

With the scribe opened to about half the diameter of the log to be notched (the actual scribe opening corresponds to the gap between the logs), start at points A and trace the curvature of the lower log, marking the upper log as you go. It is important to keep the scribe level all the way around the curve. Most logsmiths attach a small level to the scribe to ensure even marking.

The quality of the finished notch relies in large part on the accuracy of the scribing, so take the time to do it right.

scribe

Scribe opening is equal to the gap between the logs. Small level attached to scribe wing increases the accuracy of marking.

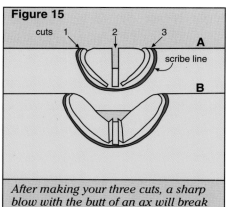

Figure 15

cuts 1 2 3   A

scribe line

B

After making your three cuts, a sharp blow with the butt of an ax will break out the two sections (A). Stay back from the scribe line about ½". The remainder of the wood is removed with hand tools—mallet and gouge, and/or a chisel (B).

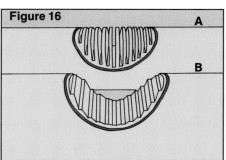

Figure 16   A

B

Make a series of cuts with the chainsaw down to within ½" of the scribe line (A). Break out the wood with the butt of an ax or hammer. Finish removing wood with hand tools (B). Some logsmiths use the tip of the chainsaw to cut away the inner portion of the wood. Remember: It takes experience to make an accurate notch with a chainsaw.

maximum accuracy the scribe must be kept level all the way around the curve. Most logsmiths attach a level to the upper scribe wing and use it to help guide the work. (See Chapter One.)

Once the log section has been marked, lay it on the ground or on blocks, scribe line up. Obviously, the quality of the notch from this point depends on the care taken in cutting it out. Treat the scribe line as sacrosanct: *Never* cut through it or outside of it, unless a preliminary fit reveals that additional wood must be removed.

The notch can be cut out in a variety of ways, with a variety of tools. Some of the very best notches I've seen were made entirely with hand tools: a wood mallet, gouge, adz, and chisel. Many logsmiths use only the chainsaw, while others use the saw for rough-forming and hand tools for finishing. Some even use an ax, but, in my opinion, unless you're a pro, an ax is not a good tool to use on a quality notch; it's simply too easy to make a misstroke and ruin the work. Probably the best method employs a combination of the chainsaw and hand tools.

Here are two ways to tackle the task:

1. Make three cuts with the chainsaw or handsaw as shown in Figure 15. Using the butt of the ax, strike the center cut

at a sharp angle; that section should break out. Then knock out the remaining section. Now, use a mallet and gouge and/or chisel to cut away the remaining wood. The tip of the chainsaw can also be used to cut away the remaining wood. Near the notch edge, use a hammer and chisel and cut right down to the scribe line, but not through it. Finally, cup or hollow out the inner portion of the notch. The upturned notch should look like a bowl, with a mid-depth of ½ to 1 inch. The area along the scribe line should be fairly thin so that during settling the edge wood will mash flat, forming an even, tight fit with the log below. The inner portion of the notch is cupped so that no high spots will contact the lower log and prevent the notch from resting solely along the scribe line.

2. This method takes more cutting with the saw (Figure 16). Make several cuts almost down to the scribe line, stopping ½ inch shy of the line. Knock out the sections with the butt of the ax. This rough-forms the notch quite quickly, but requires close attention not to cut through the scribe line. Next use a mallet and gouge (or chainsaw) to hollow out the notch. Then use the mallet, or hammer, and chisel to cut the notch down to the scribe line.

Turn the practice notch over and fit it to the log section. How have you done? A good notch should be so tight that a knife blade or piece of paper will not slip between the logs. Notches made this well result from careful work and patience, combined with experience. Don't be discouraged; keep trying. (If your notches fit tight the first time, congratulations! Mine didn't.)

Use the chainsaw to make scoring cuts to the scribe line for a round notch; this scribe line was darkened for the photo. Note that the scoring lines are well back from the edge of the notch. The midsections of wood will be knocked out with the butt of an ax.

This is a roughed-out notch; note that the pencil line is still visible. The notch is concave with a midpoint depth of about $^3/_4$ inch.

Logsmith Dick Quinn puts the finishing touches on a round notch. The log is up off the ground at a comfortable working height.

Many logsmiths are happy, gracious people. Here Arthur Mannix of Talkeetna stops to chat while working on a house in Talkeetna. Notice the scribe in his hand. The log on the top of the wall is only roughly fit; Mannix will give the log a final scribe-fitting.

Top-quality scribe-fit logs by Kim Blair of Nenana. Note how his logs taper outward near the top of the wall to support the eaves and roof line.

Probably the first few notches you make won't be perfect. Somewhere around the notch the fit will be sloppy. Don't throw that piece away; try again. Let's say, for example, the notch fits well everywhere but on one side, and there it has a gap of 1/4 inch. Try to correct it by rescribing the entire notch on both sides with a scribe setting equal to the gap. Set the scribe to the opening and carefully make a new scribe line. Turn the section over and cut down to the new scribe line with the hammer and chisel. Now try that fit. Some gaps, especially those at the lower edges of the notch, cannot be closed up; they simply are too wide, wider even than the log below. Rescribing like this on a log on the building isn't quite so simple because the log fits its length and a rescribe may only worsen the notch, unless the log is refitted its entire length. These practice notches are an excellent way to learn what can and can't be done to correct poor or faulty notches.

Most logsmiths use a chainsaw instead of hand tools to hollow out the notch, but novices should gain additional experience before trying this. Because the tip of the saw is used to cut away the wood, kickback is a real hazard in small, tight notches. Indeed,

some professionals use just a chainsaw to make the entire notch.

As in anything, there's really no right way to do a proper notch, but there are a bunch of wrong ways. Only experience will tell you what's best for you.

Try out these techniques, and your own ideas, before starting on the actual construction project. It'll quickly be obvious that a good notch can't be rushed. Some logsmiths, depending on log and notch size, spend an hour or more on each notch. The beginner may require more time. Once mastered, the round notch technique will join logs quickly and tightly.

One difference between the practice exercise and the actual thing has to do with finding the appropriate scribe setting. If all the logs are of uniform size, the setting will be the same, roughly half the diameter of the logs at the point where they cross. However, no lot of logs will ever be exactly the same size; in some cases, a wide variation in size will be the norm. A simple rule of thumb: The depth of each notch (and the distance between wing points of the scribe) is equal to the gap between the logs (Figure 17). Remember, each notch on each round of logs will vary in size and will have to be custom-fit. Take the time to do it right—you won't be sorry.

Quality scribe-fit logs and notches by author.

Although unusual places such as this pitch spot at the edge of the round notch are better off cleaned and carved to bare wood, I took an inordinate amount of time to achieve a tight fit.

Figure 17

Find the scribe setting (depth of the notch) by measuring the gap between the logs at the points indicated. Custom-fit each notch, resetting the scribe for each. Ideally, each notch should be close to half the diameter of the log, but in reality there can be quite substantial variations in notch depth because of the usual variation in log sizes.

atural logs can be round-notched and fitted together in three ways: in the round (whole), slabbed on two sides, or by scribe-fitting. However, even a brief description of the three methods will indicate that only two are viable options for the builder seeking quality.

Many sourdough cabins were built with the logs whole, or in the round, and except for the notches were unhewn. Instead they were spiked in place with gaps between that had to be chinked with mud, plaster, or wads of grass, moss, or ticking held in place with poles. The notches were crude and ill-fitting, not only allowing ingress of moisture, but also insects and even small animals as well. I once saw a cabin with such wide gaps between the logs that a rifle easily could have been sighted through the cracks, and a snowshoe hare pulled through for butchering.

I've also seen a few creditable cabins built with logs in the round, with the

A nicely finished notch on a sill log.

7

Walls

Because the logs I was using on this very complex building were rather small, and because the tie logs would have to also support the upper-story floor, I fit and bolted two tie logs together (sandwiching the floor joists) so the tie logs would flex as a unit, thereby equaling the strength of a 22-inch log, their combined diameter. Note the spaces cut into the one log for eventual head space over the doorways, the splines in the window openings, and the electrical outlet openings.

notches nicely done and the high spots between the logs removed with an ax or chainsaw, allowing for a fairly tight fit. Some of these cabins were chinked with moss, others with fiberglass. Nonetheless, heat loss remained unacceptably high. Probably the only time building with logs in the round is viable is in a remote area where you must use local timber that is too small to hew into two-sided logs or to scribe-fit together. (Actually, no log is too small to scribe-fit. The drawback would be a scarcity of timber, requiring logs to be fit whole for maximum height per round.)

Two-sided logs may be the easiest for a novice to work with, since once the logs are slabbed, all that remains is notching. A two-sided log is a natural log that has had bearing surfaces milled on two sides. After the logs are notched together, the bearing surfaces fit smoothly and neatly together. Besides being quick, neat, and simple, this method actually increases the effective insulation value of the log. The major drawback of two-sided-log construction is that, unless the outside space between the logs is sealed with oakum and/or caulk, moisture can soak between the logs into the insulation and stand on the flat surfaces long enough for mold to form and decay to begin.

Many fine-quality homes and buildings have been constructed of two-sided logs. Indeed, many expert logsmiths use two-sided logs and would build no other way. Master logsmith Paul Smith of Cooper Landing turns out some of the finest examples of two-sided-log

construction found anywhere in Alaska.

The third and best way to fit logs is with the scribe-fit technique, also called chinkless or Scandinavian style. Essentially, the log is notched its entire length to form-fit the log below. This is one of the oldest methods of log construction, coming to North America with pioneer settlers. Although called the Scandinavian style, where some 600-year-old scribe-fit buildings are still in use, examples of this technique can be found throughout Europe.

A round-notched, scribe-fit log offers unequaled protection from the elements. Done correctly, water runs off, not into, the logs; air leaks are nil; and the insulation is totally hidden from view. Thus, a tight scribe-fit seals in the heat and keeps out the cold. Even crooked logs can be utilized to good advantage. The main drawback to scribe-fitting logs is that some degree of proficiency is required to do the work properly, so for novices, this method may take more time than two-sided-log construction. However, an expert can scribe-fit logs as fast, if not faster, than another can fit two-sided logs.

Many fine logsmiths now build solely with the scribe-fit technique. Indeed, there seems to be a renaissance of this ancient skill in Alaska. When questioned, most builders say not only is the scribe-fit method superior to any other, but it offers immeasurable rewards in terms of handcraftsmanship—pride in building in the time-honored, quality way.

However, because squared logs or

three-sided logs properly belong to timber construction rather than log construction, I included them along with other styles and methods in Chapter Five. Here, I'll go into the details of two-sided and scribe-fit log building, then describe features common to both, as well as to other types of log construction.

First let's look at our sample project. The foundation is in, and the subfloor is nailed down. We're building from a platform frame, and the logs are piled on the site. We're about ready to do logwork. Should we peel all the logs first, or should we peel as we go? Either way, if building with green logs and the project will be completed in one season; otherwise, peel all. I like to peel two to four rounds of logs (8 to 16 logs), fit them on the walls, then peel more, and so on. This method varies the work, reduces the monotony, and gives the best possible protection to the logs in the stack.

If you choose to peel the whole stack at once, fight the temptation to do a hurried job. Do work as good on the last few as on the first; the finished quality depends on it. If like most cheechakos you cut and haul your own logs, brush and clear the site, then peel all the logs at once, you're bound to feel sentenced to hard labor. At one point or another, you'll swear to "never build another cabin." That's only natural, but may not prove to be accurate in the long run. Only by putting this part of yourself into the project, however, will real meaning and satisfaction come from it.

The inspired craftsmanship of Homer's Carl Jones is apparent in this beautiful, complex design.

Paul Smith of Cooper Landing mills the bearing surface of a log with a Homelite chainsaw and a 700 series Alaskan chainsaw mill. The level attached to the mill allows for an even cut. Note the oil can in his hand—extra oil for the tip of the saw—and the ear protectors. Below, the results: milled two-sided logs ready for construction.

Two-sided Logs

A log can be slabbed, or two-sided, in any number of ways. Some local mills will two-side logs on contract, but since they usually cut too much, rendering the log into a relatively thin log-board, you are better off making your own two-sided logs. Granberg's Alaskan MK III chainsaw mill is an excellent tool for this. Paul Smith, among others, uses it to precut all of his house logs. By doing his own, Smith makes the best use of each log, wasting little. However, the Alaskan mill may be too expensive for the one-time builder.

A mini-mill, such as the Haddon Lumber/Maker, is a less expensive attachment that can be used to slab logs. It may not be quite as accurate as the Alaskan mill, but in the hands of an expert, it comes close, although it's never as fast.

To slab a log using the Haddon Lumber/Maker, nail a guide board to the top of the log and adjust the attachment to the guide board. Starting at one end, cut a slab off the length of the log. Remove only enough of the curvature to fashion a 4- to 5-inch bearing surface. Adjust the guide, if necessary, and repeat the process on the opposite side, being careful to make sure the cuts are parallel and not angled off. If done correctly, you will have a two-sided log. A mill is not only the quickest way to slab logs, but also the safest, since all the logs can be slabbed on the ground before being hoisted onto the wall.

An alternate method of putting whole logs on the wall and then fashioning the bearing surfaces is fast, but not as accurate, and definitely not without risk. Put the log on the wall and roll it until you find the side you want down, usually the straightest. Mark it, then roll the log until the marks are up. Block or dog the log securely in place. Imagine a 4- to 5-inch bearing surface on the marked side. Run the chalkline the length of the log coinciding with the imagined edge of the bearing surface. Pull the line taut and snap it. Using the line as a guide, slab-flat the log with an adz, ax, or chainsaw (Figure 18). This requires good hand-eye coordination since the chalkline serves as a visual reference only, and nothing, save the skill of the logsmith, prevents the bearing surface from varying along its length, with high and low spots possible.

Roll the log over with the flat side down. Notch the log into position and you're ready to slab the topside in the same manner. The bearing surfaces of logs sided like this should contact fairly evenly, but due to the inherent

Wearing his cowboy hat, Mike Potts mills Steve Ahnert's logs into three-sided logs with his Mobile Dimension Saw at Eagle.

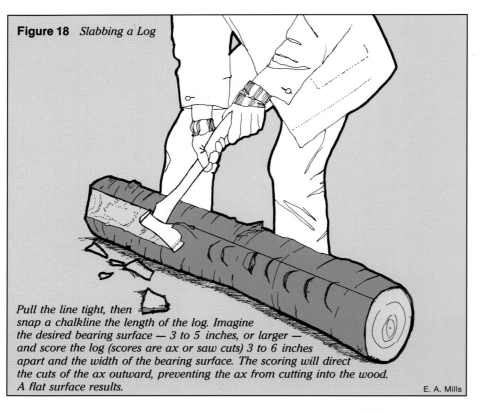

Figure 18 *Slabbing a Log*

Pull the line tight, then snap a chalkline the length of the log. Imagine the desired bearing surface — 3 to 5 inches, or larger — and score the log (scores are ax or saw cuts) 3 to 6 inches apart and the width of the bearing surface. The scoring will direct the cuts of the ax outward, preventing the ax from cutting into the wood. A flat surface results.

E. A. Mills

David Rhode drilling rebar holes. Remember: Never drive anything into untapped logs. See Figure 19.

inaccuracy of the technique, high spots usually remain to be whittled down before the logs can come together, with the notches fitting correctly. (A peavey or cant hook comes in very handy for maneuvering logs on the wall.)

The first few logs on the wall, slabbed in this alternate method, are not particularly difficult to work with, but as the wall goes up and the work proceeds from a scaffold, things become a bit more difficult and dangerous, especially the last few logs. When maneuvering a log on the wall, exercise caution. *Never, never* get between the log and the outside of the building. If the log should roll off and you're in the way . . . well, the results could be most unpleasant.

It's a matter of personal preference whether you slab all the logs prior to beginning the cabin, or do a few at a time as you progress. When building with two-sided logs, I prefer to use a chainsaw mill to slab my own logs, although I have done it a number of ways. I start by slabbing half my logs and doing the rest as I go. In perfect weather, with all the logs milled prior to start-up, a 16-foot-by-18-foot cabin does not take long to build, but perfect weather is somewhere else besides Alaska. I don't like to work on a wall when it is pouring rain; even the heaviest log will slip off the wall then, just as if it's been greased. So, on rainy days, I slab logs with the mill, with both feet flat on the ground.

Now, let's begin putting up two-sided logs. Since we're building on a platform, we'll need two half-logs to start. Select a large-diameter, slabbed, 20-foot end log, and use the chainsaw mill to halve the log lengthwise. If you don't have a mill attachment, snap a chalkline down the middle of one unhewn side, and use it as an eyeball guide for the chainsaw. Use as large a two-sided log as possible. Hopefully, you can use both halves. The butts of wall logs will be notched over these half-logs, so it is important to have large enough half-logs to allow the wall logs to be notched half their thickness. Sometimes it's necessary to cut two logs somewhat fuller than half their thickness in order to have two suitable end logs. Also, allowing 4 extra feet for notching and projection, the end log on a 16-foot-by-18-foot cabin measures 20 feet in length; the wall log, 22 feet.

No matter which technique you use, two-sided or scribe-fit, working on a platform, the first end logs must always be half-logs.

Now put the half-logs in place. If you have rebars (steel reinforcing rod) or bolts sticking up through the floor, drill the half-logs and set them down over the ties. Remember: Always drill the logs first; never drive anything into untapped logs. Spikes pounded into logs will undo all you've worked so hard to achieve. Instead of pulling logs together, spikes will hold them apart as they dry and settle, causing gaps and cracks to form between them.

Before driving anything into the logs, use a ¹/₂-inch or ⁵/₈-inch bit (a ship's auger works best) to drill through the top log and halfway into the log below.

openings. This way the logs will settle on the pins without binding, and the heads will not stick up, keeping the logs apart. I prefer to use wooden pegs instead of metal, because if I miscalculate their location, or later add on to or modify the cabin, I won't have to worry about contacting metal with the saw.

There are two ways to begin the sequence of fitting logs. In one, the butts of the two half-logs face the same direction. Then the butts of the first two wall logs, also facing the same direction but toward the front of the cabin, are notched over the half-logs. If you've calculated correctly, the wall logs will be notched half their thickness and the entire joinery process will have begun.

One wall log will be notched at both ends over the butts of the two half-logs; the other wall log will be notched over the top ends of the half-logs (Figure 20A).

Several logsmiths would disagree here, offering a different beginning. Some begin by alternating ends, the butts of the half-logs facing the opposite directions. For example, the rear end log's butt extends to the left, the front end log's butt to the right. Then the wall logs go down, also with the butts alternating, the left one's butt to the back, the right wall log's butt to the front (Figure 20B). In this manner, on the initial round, unlike the first method, tops will be notched over tops and butts over butts, thereby eliminating

---

Figure 19 *Drilled holes for countersinking pegs or rebars*

Before driving anything into the logs, use a 1/2-inch or 5/8-inch ship's auger to drill through the top log and halfway into the log below. Then, using a 3/4-inch or 1-inch bit, drill down 4 inches into each hole.

¾" or 1" auger hole

4" hole counter-sunk to receive spike

¹/₂" or ⁵/₈" auger hole

minimum of half-log's diameter

Then, using a ³/₄-inch or 1-inch bit, drill down 4 inches into each of these holes (Figure 19). Now a spike (10 to 13 inches), rebar, or dry wooden peg can be countersunk into the holes. Make sure it fits loosely. Place the pins at 4-foot intervals along the log. On small cabins, place pins on each end of the log, in from the notch about a foot, and on either side of window and door

---

Figure 20 *The First Round*

There are two ways of beginning the sequence of fitting logs. In one (A) the butts of the two half-logs face the same direction. In the other (B), tops will be notched over tops, and butts over butts.

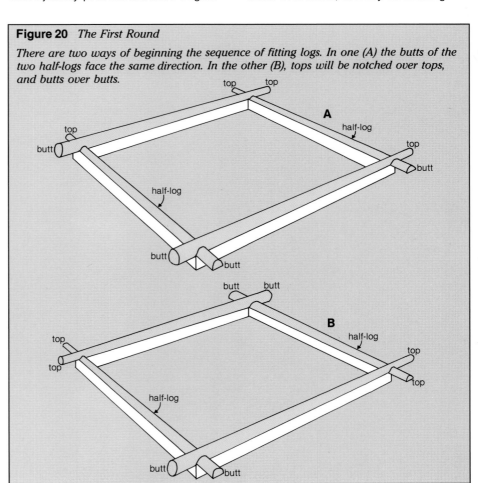

the problem of trying to notch a too-small top over the large butt end.

I prefer the first technique, however, mainly because on the last round, when the caplogs go on the wall, the butts *both* face to the front. To me, nothing looks better than a cabin with the large butts of sturdy caplogs, purlins, and ridgepole pointing forward, overhanging the porch. Alternating ends as in the second technique defeats this, since one caplog will present a top looking like a toothpick in comparison to the other roof supports. This can be corrected by setting the one caplog on the wall out of sequence, the butt forward, instead of to the rear. But if you're not careful, that may set the wall height way off.

Some logsmiths have developed formulas for notching, calculating log notch depth, and so on, but I prefer a simpler approach. Do what works best for you, and don't be dismayed if things don't always work out perfectly. Every logsmith makes mistakes, so go ahead and build; that's how we all started, by doing. Experience is the best teacher. One reason for using a small 16-foot-by-

18-foot cabin as an example is so you can build one too, gaining experience and knowledge before beginning a more complex structure.

Once the first round is on the building and pinned in place, the rest of the wall construction becomes mostly repetition. No matter which beginning sequence you use, you must alternate ends as you go up, butt-top, butt-top, to keep the walls level. When using two-sided logs, tight notches are the most important detail and are examples of your craftsmanship. A good scribe helps a lot, but so does experience. Always measure the gap between the bearing surfaces of the logs, inside the corner, never toward the midpoint of the log, as logs do sag somewhat. Set the scribe about 1/4 inch smaller than the measured gap. That way, if you make a mistake, the error will hopefully be on the conservative side, the notch smaller than needed, not bigger. Scribe both notches of a log, with custom scribe settings. Measure the gap at each inside corner, and set the scribe accordingly. If the notches are a shade too small and the bearing surfaces don't come

into contact, rescribe both notches, using the new measured gap setting. Recut the notch and check it. If it fits, you're finished and ready to insulate and pin the logs together. Should the notches fit poorly, with gaps, but the bearing surfaces fit tightly, your only way of correcting this is to cut the entire bearing surface down and redo the notches. You may or may not want to rehew the log. It just depends on how much slop you want to tolerate.

Unlike the scribe-fit method, where all insulation is hidden from view, insulation can be seen between two-sided logs. Fiberglass sill-sealer, in ready-cut 4-inch-wide rolls, seems the best log insulation to use. Always use yellow (not red or pink) sill-sealer, as it matches the color of the logs. Staple it to the bottom log and turn the top log down on it. Be neat and cut off or tuck in any ragged or unduly exposed sections of insulation.

Each round of logs goes up the same way. Pin and drill the logs as you go. Build a sturdy scaffold inside to work from, and take your time. Tight notches and well-fit logs can't be hurried. (See Figure 21.)

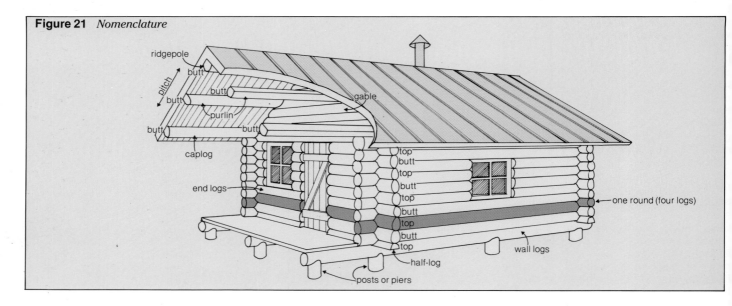

Figure 21 *Nomenclature*

Scribe-Fit

While this so-called chinkless method of log joinery usually takes more time than two-sided log construction, it offers superior weather-resistance. A major concern, however, is that scribe-fit logs definitely shrink more than two-sided logs. (There's just no such thing as dry logs; all logs will shrink to varying degrees.) Close attention must be paid to design and construction features that consider this fact.

Before the advent of chainsaws, logs were hewn with hand tools. Notches were cut with the ax, adz, scorp, and chisel. The scribe log trough, or what I call the lateral groove, was fashioned with the adz. Power saws speeded the work immensely and, instead of being U-shaped, the lateral groove became V-shaped.

The whole idea of scribe-fitting is to match the upper log to the shape of the lower log. The scribe, one with a double level attachment, becomes an important, almost indispensable tool here. With it, the logsmith transfers the shape and contour of the bottom log onto the upper log. Thus, the quality of the scribe has a great deal to do with the efficiency and speed with which this work can be done. In essence, we are making a log-long notch, with the top log being notched to fit not only at the corners, but to the entire length of the log below. The log obviously cannot be hewn any better than it is marked. (Since the top portion of every log remains round and intact, with the notches and groove on the down side, all moisture runs off the logs.)

To build walls by scribe-fitting, begin with half-logs on the ends, then notch the first wall logs over them. The sequence, or pattern of laying logs, and the initial start-up is no different than for two-sided logs.

Place the first whole end log directly above and parallel to the half-log, butts reversed (butt above top, top above butt). If the log has a slight bow to it, roll the log so that the bow is down. With slightly bowed logs, or those with "whale-back," it is sometimes advantageous to drawknife the hump or bow until the log is fairly straight, although that's not always

With the log rough-notched into place, Dick Quinn scribes the lateral groove of the entire log.

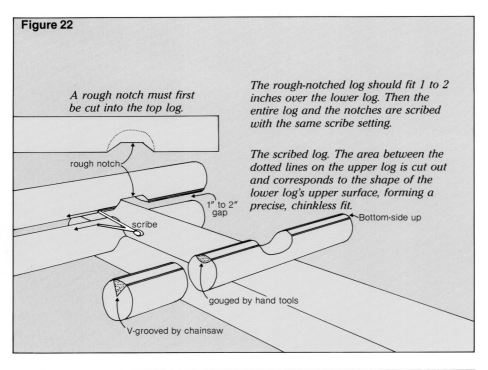

Figure 22

A rough notch must first be cut into the top log.

rough notch

1" to 2" gap

scribe

The rough-notched log should fit 1 to 2 inches over the lower log. Then the entire log and the notches are scribed with the same scribe setting.

The scribed log. The area between the dotted lines on the upper log is cut out and corresponds to the shape of the lower log's upper surface, forming a precise, chinkless fit.

Bottom-side up

gouged by hand tools

V-grooved by chainsaw

This wall was pieced together to make the best use of the fewest number of logs. The windows have been cut out and now the full-length header log is being fitted. Note the cable and boom truck that put the log in place. A scaffold is a necessity on larger buildings; the 2x4 prop inside is to steady the section between the windows and hold it in place for scribing.

possible with badly bowed logs. Use log dogs or blocks to hold the log in position. Scribe the preliminary notches. These rough notches should be deep enough so that the log will set down to within 2 inches of the log below. To set the scribe, measure the gap between the logs and subtract 2 inches: Use that measure.

Roll the log over and cut out the rough notches. When the log is turned back into position, it will rest 1 or 2 inches above the log below (Figure 22).

Now set the scribe slightly larger than the widest space between the logs. Use this one setting for the entire log. Carefully keeping the scribe level, mark the corner notches and scribe both sides of the log its entire length, including those portions outside the notches (Figure 22). Use an indelible pencil to mark the scribe line. For a precise, tight fit, the scribe marks must be accurate. Check the lines by going over them lightly a second time. Make sure the scribe adjustment is tight and doesn't loosen during use, giving a faulty, varying mark.

The whole idea of scribing is that the two parallel lines traced by the scribe are a constant vertical distance apart. Once the wood is cut away on the upper log, it will fit precisely to the lows and highs of the lower log.

Roll the log over. The two parallel lines correspond exactly to the shape of the lower log. To begin hewing, first cut out the notches as described in Chapter Six. Then, using the tip of the chainsaw, follow the lines and cut out a V-shaped groove (U-shaped if using hand tools) the length of the log (Figure 22). Be careful not to cut through the scribe line. For the best results, make the initial saw cut 1/4 inch back inside from the line; after roughing out the groove with the saw or adz, finish up to the edge with a slick or chisel. On a 16-by-18-foot cabin, it may take a novice four hours or more to properly notch and fit a single end log, perhaps longer if only hand tools are used. Don't hurry the work, though: Speed will come with proficiency.

Some logsmiths disdain the use of a chainsaw for shaping the lateral groove, pointing out that too much wood can be wasted, and this "gutting" only

Dick Quinn uses a Homelite chainsaw to cut along the scribe line. A professional like Dick can cut close to the line, but a beginner would be well-advised to stay farther away from it.

Next, Dick uses the tip of the saw to smooth out the lateral groove on a scribe-fit log. Note the ear protectors.

Once both sides of the lateral groove are cut, scoring cuts between them are made with a chainsaw. The sections are then chopped out with an adz.

In this photo, the scoring cuts have been partially removed; note the adz on the ground. The groove is shallow and cupped.

Both notches and the lateral groove have been roughed out and will now be cleaned and prepared for fitting.

exacerbates the shrinkage factor. Many prefer to use hand tools, shunning the V-shape for the traditional U-shape of the adz-hewn lateral groove (Figure 22). One Southeastern logsmith says, with some vehemence, that the final interior portion of the lateral groove should clear the log below by no more than 1/2 inch. Others disagree, saying that this degree of perfection is unnecessary and that the time is better spent elsewhere. However, whether you use hand tools or power tools, one thing is certain: The lateral groove should not be cut any deeper than necessary, usually less than one-fourth the log thickness. The deeper the groove, the greater the shrinkage will be.

After hewing the notches and lateral groove, roll the log into place and check the fit. Done expertly, a knife blade will not fit anywhere between the logs. If the notches or groove fit poorly, the scribe line probably wasn't accurate.

Occasionally the lines will be accurate and the log will be resting on high spots inside the groove. Check that first. If not, the only way to correct for gaps is to rescribe the entire log, notches included. If, for example, the notches fit fine but there are 1/4-inch gaps where the two logs contact, set the scribe to the largest gap size, 1/4 inch, and rescribe the entire log. Professional logsmiths can sometimes lay 80% of the logs in a building with only one scribe. Other times it may take two or three scribes to get the logs tight. Try to keep your notches about half the thickness of the log you're working on. Sometimes the notches will be deeper, but avoid it if possible.

I once fit 13 logs in a row with just one scribe per log. Feeling pretty confident, I was shown up by number 14, which took four scribes to fit. Four hours later, on the last go-round, the scribe setting measured 1/16 inch. I was getting even.

Once satisfied with the fit, roll the log up and loosely fill the groove with insulation. Stuff the concave part of the notch as well. Regardless of the nickname, chinkless logs do need this insulation. Roll the log into position and pin it into place. Fit the remaining wall logs in the same manner.

Satisfied with the fit, Dick Quinn insulates a log with sill-sealer.

If you're having trouble making the logs fit, check for inside contact by slipping a piece of paper through the gaps and feeling for contact. Remove these high spots first before deciding to rescribe the log. The key is in using a good scribe to make accurate scribe lines. With a double bubble attachment, accuracy is assured if the scribe is held level while marking the log. Sometimes the scribed log will ride up on the log below because high spots just inside of the scribe line are contacting the lower log, rather than the log contacting only at the scribe line.

And, finally, be patient. Sometimes it just takes two or three scribes to get the log to fit right. Not everyone can finish a log with just one scribe. Practice will improve your ability and knowledge.

Whether you are working with scribe-fit or two-sided logs, it is important to keep parallel walls going up evenly. Most logsmiths try to maintain the same wall height on *even* rounds. For example, with two wall logs in place, the height up from the floor at *each* corner should be roughly the same. The measurements at rounds 6, 8, and 10 should also be even. Obviously, since butts and tops are alternated, the odd rounds will be higher at the butt end of the log than at the top end. When setting the even rounds, try to maintain the same height. Depending on log size, most cabin walls stand about 10 rounds high. Of course this varies according to individual plans, but 10 seems to be average. Always build the walls a minimum of 6 inches higher than desired. For example, if your plans call for 8-foot walls, build them 8 feet, 6 inches. Over two or three years the walls will settle to about 8 feet.

The last, or top, wall logs are called caplogs. From the five extra-long roof supports that you've set aside, select the best for the ridgepole, then pick two appropriate logs for the caplogs. This'll be your last chance to even out the wall height. Even though you've measured the walls as you've worked, juggling log size to keep the walls roughly even, you'll not always come out perfect. By using different-diameter caplogs you may be able to match up the walls. Hopefully the finished walls, with the caplogs in place, will be of the same height. If not, 1/2 inch or less variation, while not desirable, will not make that much difference or adversely affect the roof construction.

Besides coming out even, the walls

should be plumb. About the time the first round of logs goes on the building, it's necessary to decide which way to plumb the walls. A common method, and the one that produces a pleasing interior wall surface, lines up the inside edges of the logs (Figure 23A). A simple carpenter's square and level, used with a board or straightedge, is used to plumb the wall. As each log is placed on the wall, use the tools to keep it in line. Some logsmiths like to plumb the outside of the wall (23C), merely a cosmetic touch, and others plumb the logs on a center line (23B), which makes more sense because you end up with a uniform wall, inside and out. (Using the scribe-fit technique, it's best to plumb the logs on a center line.)

Trimming the exterior log ends can wait until the cabin is complete, or it can be done as the logs go up. If you want staggered or pointed ends (Figure 24A and B), the cuts have to be made as you go. If the logs are to be cut square (Figure 24C), they should be trimmed all at the same time, using a chalkline as a cutting guide. Never cut the ends too short; always leave plenty of overhang. A cabin with log ends cut short looks narrow and unsturdy. Some builders leave the last round or two of wall logs long to support the caplogs, an effective way of preventing the caplog from bowing under snow loads.

If the cabin is to be wired for electricity, it's best to drill each round of logs, pulling the wiring up through as you go. Some logsmiths lay two to three rounds of logs, then, using a long bit and extension, drill down through the layers. Then they push the wiring up from underneath or down from the top. I prefer to tap each round as I go. On some cabins, I've run all the wiring through the door and window splines, with no extra drilling for the wiring. Openings for switches and outlets can be cut into the logs with a drill and chisels or with specially adapted tools. Logsmith Brian Forbes has a specially made bar—a sculptor's bar—for his chainsaw, which allows him to cut the square outlets and switch box openings without the chainsaw kicking back.

Your plan, besides showing the electric layout, will, of course, indicate

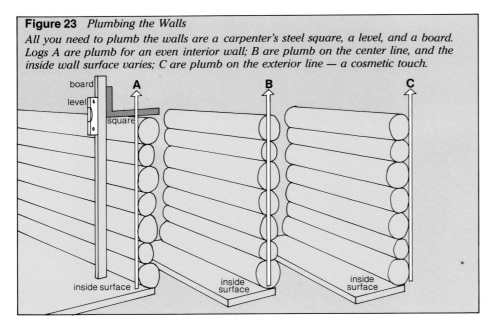

Figure 23 *Plumbing the Walls*
All you need to plumb the walls are a carpenter's steel square, a level, and a board. Logs A are plumb for an even interior wall; B are plumb on the center line, and the inside wall surface varies; C are plumb on the exterior line — a cosmetic touch.

board
level
square
A
B
C
inside surface
inside surface
inside surface

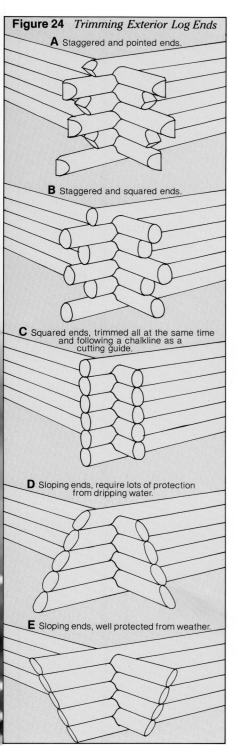

Figure 24 *Trimming Exterior Log Ends*

A Staggered and pointed ends.

B Staggered and squared ends.

C Squared ends, trimmed all at the same time and following a chalkline as a cutting guide.

D Sloping ends, require lots of protection from dripping water.

E Sloping ends, well protected from weather.

the exact location of doors and windows. This is important not only for locating the wiring, but for proper placement of wall pins. If possible, use full-length logs on small buildings. Cut the doors and windows out after the walls are up. I usually leave a rough door opening as I build since it makes for easier access to the interior. On large cabins or homes it may be necessary to use short lengths of logs to piece the walls together, leaving gaps at openings. If so, always use full-length logs above and below window openings. Avoid splices. Note: If you want large windows or sliding doors, you can build cheaper, buying fewer logs, if you piece the wall together, so plan carefully.

(Cutting and supporting window and door openings, plus pointers on piecing logs, are covered in the next chapter.)

Small log buildings, such as our sample, do not need interior cross support. However, larger cabins, with walls longer than 25 feet, need a tie log. The tie log should span the center of the building and be notched over the last wall log, with the caplog notched over that. For your tie log, pick a fairly straight log with just a slight bow in it. Fit the tie log on the building with the bow up. Logs supported only at the ends will eventually succumb to gravity and sag, but with the bow up, the result will be a level log.

To cut an opening for an electric box, drill two holes in the log face to the depth of the box. Next chisel around the holes and inset the electric box. Drill a hole down through the logs and floor so that the electrical wiring can come up into the box. Sand the opening smooth. In this case, the wiring will run up through the door spline mortise and into the back of the box.

Builder Sandy Jamieson (left) uses the peavey while helpful homeowner Frank Entsminger drives rebar. Just beating the arrival of winter, they are working on the gables. (Sue Entsminger)

As the walls grow higher, it becomes more and more difficult to work with the logs. A simple scaffold built on the inside of the cabin will greatly aid the work. However, getting the logs up onto the walls sometimes can be a problem. On very small cabins, two persons can lift small logs into place. On larger buildings, one person can lift logs using skids and a come-along (Figure 25). Tie a rope to the log so that the cable attaches to the balance point of the log. Then simply crank the log up onto the wall.

Chainsaw-engine-powered winches are available, and some folks use them to move logs. Personally, I'd never use one of my saw engines that way. Chainsaws are made to cut wood, not winch heavy logs. But if you decide one would be worthwhile, I recommend purchasing a second power plant to use just for that purpose.

Frankly, I think a come-along could accomplish any task a mini-winch could, though perhaps not as effortlessly. I've set a 24-foot ridgepole in place, 18 feet off the ground, using nothing more than a hand winch and rope.

Many professionals use power hoists to lift logs. Some employ A-frames and winches mounted on 4x4s, or heavy equipment. Others use cranes or hydraulic lifts. For most of us, however, such large pieces of equipment are not affordable.

A gin pole might be the best setup for one person to lift logs. Basically, a gin pole is a boom and fulcrum set inside the building. The boom is lowered, usually by block and tackle or hand winch, and the log to be lifted is attached. The boom is then raised and the whole assembly—boom, upright, and log—swivels on a pivot. The log is then lowered into the desired position (Figure 26).

No matter how you hoist your logs, keep spectators and helpers well away from the work area. Never, under any circumstances, allow anyone to stand below or near moving logs. Should the rope or cable part, the log would slam down with potentially lethal force. Also, when working logs on the building, always stand *inside*, never outside the log. If the log should roll off the wall

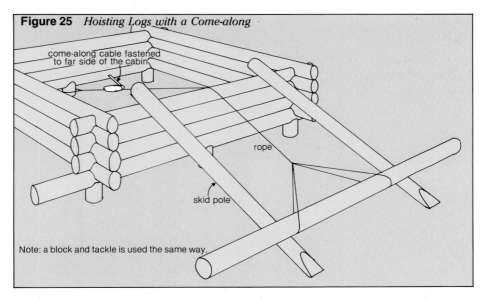

Figure 25 *Hoisting Logs with a Come-along*

come-along cable fastened to far side of the cabin

rope

skid pole

Note: a block and tackle is used the same way.

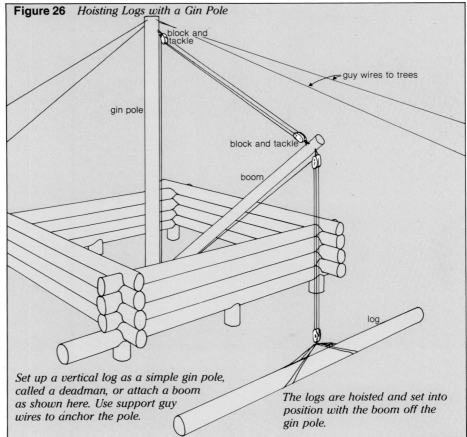

Figure 26 *Hoisting Logs with a Gin Pole*

block and tackle

guy wires to trees

gin pole

block and tackle

boom

log

Set up a vertical log as a simple gin pole, called a deadman, or attach a boom as shown here. Use support guy wires to anchor the pole.

The logs are hoisted and set into position with the boom off the gin pole.

This gin pole and boom for the construction of a log house at Chinulna Point near Kenai was set up by Tom Corr Jr. of Soldotna.

and you're in the way, it could crush you or take you hurtling over the edge.

If this is your first cabin and if you do the work carefully, it may go up quite slowly, especially if you are working alone. There'll be some point when every long day's work looks the same, progress frustratingly hard to detect. Then is the time to take extra care. If things go bad and you feel they're getting worse, sit down and take a break or, better yet, go hunting or fishing for the day. Don't get in a hurry. Remember, you're building with logs. I never said

the work would go fast; on the contrary, I've said the opposite. So how long will it take to put up the walls? However long it takes. Alone, an expert logsmith can put up a 16-foot-by-18-foot cabin in ten days, depending on a variety of factors and design features. A month, more accurately. A novice, striving to achieve the same quality, might take an entire summer. The whole concept of log building calls for patience and hard work—the ingredients to lasting quality and craftsmanship, things sadly vanishing in the modern world.

This is me maneuvering a 44-foot wall log onto the building with my hydraulic truck.

Few old cabins, especially sourdough relics, have many windows, usually just two or three small ones, and inside they are often as dark as solitary confinement—which wouldn't be a half-bad description of wintering in one. For the most part, their builders—prospectors, trappers, traders—stayed quite active outside, returning to the cabin to eat and sleep or seek refuge from the cold. Some sourdoughs, especially in the early dark part of winter, hibernated like bears, sleeping away the days in Olympic-class style. Who needs windows to sleep 16 hours a day?

More obvious reasons included the practical desire to minimize heat loss and the very real scarcity of glass or substitute material. Glass wasn't available in the bush, and had to be transported by steamship, riverboat, and eventually hand, reaching only those who were accessible and wealthy enough to pay.

Even today, however, cabins go up with only a few windows, the dim interiors ranking right along with those earlier bear dens. We hear much of cabin fever, and many things contribute to it, but who wouldn't feel confined and claustrophobic in a nearly windowless cabin in country where in winter the sun makes only a feeble appearance for a few hours a day, if it shines at all? (Lack of access may be the one sourdough-era excuse valid today for not putting in *glass* windows, but inexpensive, unbreakable substitutes abound.) True, top-quality framed windows can be astronomically expensive, but plain glass isn't. If you can build a cabin, you can build your own windows, and cheaply. And by using double or triple panes, heat loss becomes insignificant.

Doors and Windows

Frank and Sue Entsminger's home near the Little Tok River in the Mentasta Mountains was built by Sandy and Bruce Jamieson of Fairbanks. The framing above the window serves as a covering over the settling space to prevent squirrels from getting into the cabin, yet does not hinder the settling. The logs are finished with CWF (Clear Wood Finish) and clear latex on the log ends to preserve whiteness.

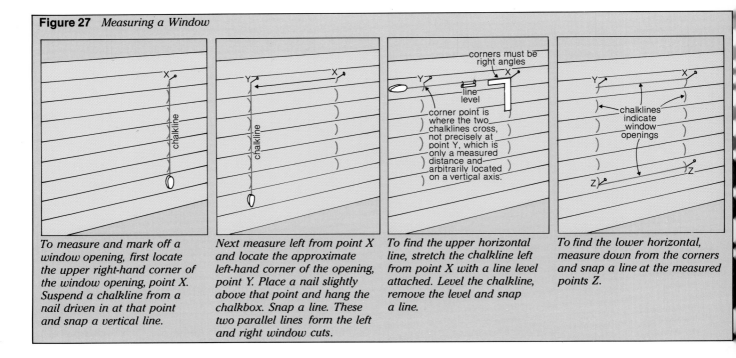

Figure 27 *Measuring a Window*

To measure and mark off a window opening, first locate the upper right-hand corner of the window opening, point X. Suspend a chalkline from a nail driven in at that point and snap a vertical line.

Next measure left from point X and locate the approximate left-hand corner of the opening, point Y. Place a nail slightly above that point and hang the chalkbox. Snap a line. These two parallel lines form the left and right window cuts.

To find the upper horizontal line, stretch the chalkline left from point X with a line level attached. Level the chalkline, remove the level and snap a line.

To find the lower horizontal, measure down from the corners and snap a line at the measured points Z.

So go ahead and install good-size windows, taking full advantage of sunlight and exposure. Locate your windows over such prime work areas as the table and kitchen counter. Plan in advance and have a firm idea of placement before construction.

Rough openings must be cut larger than the framed window. If the windows are placed in openings cut exactly to size, within 12 months or so, the glass most likely will be broken and the frame twisted by settling of the logs. Adequate settling space must be left above *every* opening. In some instances, on log homes built with large logs, I've left 6 inches of space above the windows. Over a period of two years, the owners watched the openings close up and fit tightly to the frames. The logsmith, unlike the framer, must constantly plan for and cope with this inevitable settling and shrinkage, especially when using scribe-fit logs. One builder says that it takes five years for a log structure to completely settle.

Because of settling, door openings cannot be cut exactly to finish size either. Instead, the rough opening must

be cut larger than standard. Suppose you plan a standard 6-foot, 8-inch door You can't get by with the usual 6-foot, 10-inch rough opening. You must do additional calculation and allow for settling by leaving space above the top jamb. The rough opening will probably measure 7 feet, 2 inches or 7 feet, 4 inches.

A rule of thumb: When using logs of 8 inches or less in diameter, allow $1/2$ inch of space for each foot of wall height. For large logs over 8 inches, allow $5/8$ inch per each foot of wall height. For example, an 8-foot wall, built with small logs, requires a settling space of 4 inches above the windows and doors.

Let's say, as an example, on a 16-by-18-foot cabin built with 8-foot walls and 8-inch logs, the framed window measures 40 inches by 61 inches. The actual rough window opening will be 44 inches by $61^{1}/_{2}$ inches. Note that the length of the opening is only slightly longer than the framed window, but 4 inches higher, leaving a full 4-inch space above the window frame for settling. This gap will close up in a year or year and a half, but it is essential.

I should point out that some logs in some areas will settle more than logs from other areas. As the builder, however, you must compensate for settling regardless of material, even if you are using dead-standing or fire-killed logs. Obviously, green logs settle the most and require the most compensation.

Window openings can be cut out in several ways; whatever method you use, it is important to make the cuts square and accurate. Although an expert, using just a chalkline for reference, can cut out a window and have it come out square and true, a novice should use a saw guide to ensure a clean, accurate cut.

Figure 27 illustrates a simple way to cut out a window. Measure the window and framing material. Plan the opening $1/2$ inch longer and 3 to 5 inches higher than the finished window frame. (Use the rule of thumb to calculate exact size.) With the measurements in hand, locate the upper right-hand corner of the opening by measuring up from the floor and out from the corner of the wall the distances needed to place the window where you want it. Be accurate because the rest of the measurements will be taken from this point. Drive a nail partway into the log at the mark. Use the chalkbox and line as a plumb bob. Suspend the chalkbox from the nail and let out a length of line longer than the vertical opening measurement. When the chalkbox stops swinging, stretch the chalkline tight and snap it. This line will be perfectly vertical and true. Next, from the nail toward the left, measure the length of the window opening. Mark the spot. A few inches directly above the mark, drive in another nail. Hang the chalkbox and make another chalkline in the same manner as the first. The two vertical lines should be perfectly parallel, measuring exactly the same distance between points. Check it and adjust if necessary. Next, attach the chalkline to the right-hand nail. Stretch it to the left and attach a line level. Tighten the string and adjust the line until the bubble centers. Remove the level and snap the line. This line marks the upper window cut. Use the carpenter square to check the lines. Each corner should be a right angle. (The upper line can be located using just the square and chalkline.) To find the bottom horizontal line, measure down from the corners. Snap another line between the two verticals. Carefully check all measurements to ensure that the opening is marked square and true, and to the appropriate size.

Next, on the outside of the vertical lines, nail 2x6s. Carefully sharpen the chainsaw and cut out the window using the boards to help guide the saw. Keep the saw cutting on a straight line, being careful not to move it right or left, as this will result in an uneven cut. Knock out the loose log section. (Some logsmiths prefer to use a good crosscut saw or two-man crosscut for making window and door cuts since they cut slower and can be controlled better.)

A chainsaw attachment can also be put to good use for making window or door openings. A Haddon Lumber/Maker can greatly facilitate cutting window and door openings. Some logsmiths call the Lumber/Maker a window-guide since here it has one of its finest applications.

Attach the Lumber/Maker to the bar.

I am using a Stihl chainsaw and a Haddon Lumber/Maker to cut out a window; the attachment follows an upright 2x4. These side cuts are made prior to placing the header log in position.

Nail a guide board directly left of the chalklines. Adjust the attachment to fit the guide board. Start the saw and ease it into the logs. Cut through and then down, using the attachment to guide the saw. Because the saw cannot move and follows an exact path, the cuts turn out extremely neat and precise. The tool can also be used to make horizontal cuts, but avoid making them if possible. *Overhead cuts are dangerous!* Also use extreme caution cutting with a chainsaw in the corner of an opening: Therein lies the *greatest kickback potential found in the entire project.*

A neophyte builder would be very well-advised to plan the window openings so that the upper horizontal line corresponds to the line where two logs fit together (Figure 28). Occasionally, a window opening will fit properly between logs, making an overhead horizontal cut unnecessary; but usually, except through meticulous

Figure 28 *Cutting a Window*

Avoid making this header (or lintel) cut unless it's made before the log is permanently attached to the wall.

A

header log

jamb

sill

chalklines

B

window sill log

cuts down to chalkline

Because overhead cuts are dangerous, avoid them. Plan the window openings so that the upper horizontal line corresponds to the line where two logs fit together, or make the cut before the log is on the wall (A). Given a choice, always opt for a sill cut (B), which is easy to make. Make cuts to the chalkline, then use an ax, adz, or chainsaw to smooth the sill.

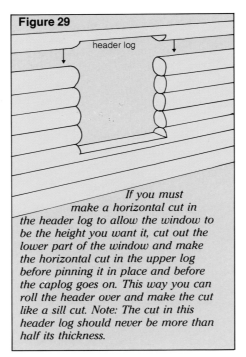

Figure 29

header log

If you must make a horizontal cut in the header log to allow the window to be the height you want it, cut out the lower part of the window and make the horizontal cut in the upper log before pinning it in place and before the caplog goes on. This way you can roll the header over and make the cut like a sill cut. Note: The cut in this header log should never be more than half its thickness.

planning, that circumstance seldom arises. Given a choice, always opt for a sill cut. Sill cuts present no unusual problems and are easy to make. To cut a sill, make cuts down to the chalkline, being careful to keep the saw level (Figure 28B). Knock out the sections and smooth the sill with the ax, adz, or chainsaw.

Usually, when I know that the window openings will require a horizontal cut in the header log, I cut out the windows before putting down the last wall or end log (Figure 29). Then I place the final log into position with the header cut already made. This way the upper horizontal cut can be made like a sill cut, avoiding the hazards and toil of overhead cutting. Always form the settling space below the caplog. Never cut through or into the caplog.

The walls on old cabins, especially relics and skeletons, often failed at window openings. The walls have bowed in or out, or even collapsed at the openings. Why? They failed because of settling. You need to cope with settling. In addition to the settling space needed

above windows and doors, extra wall reinforcement must be provided at all openings.

Left unreinforced, the logs on either side of a cut will move under the stress of settling. The best way to reinforce the wall and allow the logs to shrink and settle without hindrance or binding is to spline each opening. A spline is a wooden upright, usually a length of 2x4, mortised into the window and door jambs (Figure 30). Some builders drill 2-inch-diameter holes down through the logs 4 inches on either side of openings. (This requires exact marking of door and window openings as soon as the first round of logs goes down.) Then, after the openings are cut, the spline mortise is made by making saw cuts in the jamb down to the auger holes and removing the intervening wood.

I prefer to cut the spline mortise without these holes. Instead, I mark two parallel lines, 2 inches apart, down the center of the jamb and use a sharp

Figure 30
Reinforcing Window and Door Openings
The best way to reinforce a wall and to allow the logs to shrink and settle without binding is to spline each opening.

gap above spline to allow for settling

2" holes can be drilled as an aid to cutting spline

window opening

2x4" spline mortised into window opening

sill

Kim Blair splining a window. The tip of the saw is used to cut out a mortise in the window opening into which an upright 2x4 is placed. The cut at the upper corner is the most dangerous cut that can be made with a chainsaw on the entire project.

Settling space must be left above all doors and windows. Here the space above the door is filled with fiberglass insulation, loosely packed. The logwork, by Dick Quinn, had already settled more than 2 inches between the finish of construction and the time this photo was taken six months later.

I made this mortise cut for a window spline. The spline continues up into the header log, which will then settle over the spline itself.

The bow in this window frame was caused by the pressure of the logs on the frame—no settling space had been left above the windows. Window glass may soon break and/or the frame will twist and break if the pressure is not relieved.

chainsaw to cut out the groove. I make three 4-inch-deep cuts with the saw, being cautious at the upper corners of each—prime kickback danger zones. Then I saw out the remaining wood. To finish, I lodge a 2x4 spline in the groove, leaving settling space above it (Figure 30). The window opening is then ready for framing and finishing.

On occasion, I've cut the mortise in the door jambs 5 or 6 inches deep, instead of 4, and run the electrical wiring up through the spline mortise to the switch boxes. This works well and makes for easy manipulation of the wiring.

Once the window goes in, use sill-sealer to insulate all sides of the frame, and clear caulk to seal the cracks on the outside. Pack loose insulation in the gap above the window so that it will compress and not hinder settling. If you want to, nail a facing to the frame to hide the gap until it closes.

Some logsmiths, as an added touch, use trim or molding around the windows and doors. The molding or trim—1x4s, 1x6s, or millwork—can be fitted to the outside of the logs or inset to the window framing. Solely a matter of taste, trim isn't necessary if the jambs are cut square and neat and the window is framed with false jambs of attractive lumber. A chamfer, a cut sloped 45 degrees away from the opening, may look better than trim, adding a finishing touch of more natural appeal; or the logs can be left round.

As mentioned in the previous chapter, the walls on small cabins should go up in one piece, with the window and door openings cut out of the solid log walls. Sometimes, however, when building large log homes or structures, it isn't possible to span the required distances with a single log. In such cases, it becomes necessary to piece the walls together with short logs. This requires precise location of door and window openings. One short log reaches to a rough opening, then another completes the span. Sometimes, three or four short log sections will be used to make up one span (Figure 31). If you must err, do so on the long side, making the window

and door openings smaller than their finished size. For necessary support, always use a full-length log above and below window openings. The rough openings can be trimmed up later using techniques similar to those used for solid log walls.

Piecing together walls can be difficult. Always try to match log sections of the same diameter so that the walls, at all

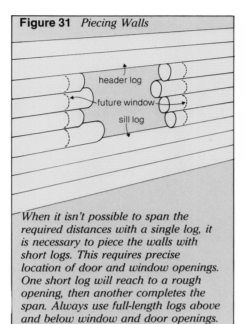

Figure 31 *Piecing Walls*

header log

future window

sill log

When it isn't possible to span the required distances with a single log, it is necessary to piece the walls with short logs. This requires precise location of door and window openings. One short log will reach to a rough opening, then another completes the span. Always use full-length logs above and below window and door openings.

points, rise at the same rate. Even if you could get by with a small-diameter section in the middle, say, and two large sections on the ends, don't. The height might be the same, but the finished span will look odd and unbalanced. Additionally, keep all wall sections plumb. Boards or poles may be needed to provide extra support.

If your plans call for large picture windows, the entire project can be completed using fewer total logs. It does make a difference. On one large home I worked on, we saved the equivalent of four large trees by using log sections. And the owner saved some money. Logs were selling for $2.99 a linear foot in that area, and his were 45-footers!

This angle cut is called a chamfer and is a neat way to finish a window opening. Basically a chamfer is a simple beveled cut back from the window frame. This logwork was done by Paul Smith.

(Top) South-facing windows in this cabin
built by Kim Blair and Jeff King take full
advantage of site and exposure.

(Bottom) Sarah Norris enters the family
home built by the late Paul Smith of
Cooper Landing. The three small
windows add a nice touch to this
south-facing wall.

Kim Blair cuts out a window using a Haddon Lumber/Maker. The jig made of 2x4s guides the cut.

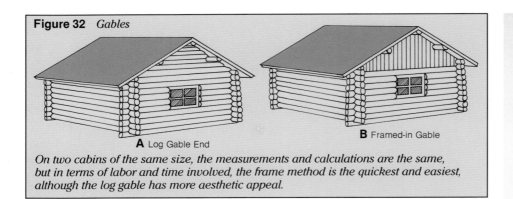

Figure 32 *Gables*

A Log Gable End   **B** Framed-in Gable

On two cabins of the same size, the measurements and calculations are the same, but in terms of labor and time involved, the frame method is the quickest and easiest, although the log gable has more aesthetic appeal.

The gable ends can be framed in or made of logs. Either method requires the same basic measurements and calculations. Log gables offer aesthetic appeal; frame gables, speed and ease of construction. I discuss both, but emphasize logwork.

The incline of the roof, called pitch, has to be decided first. Natural factors, such as snowfall and annual temperature variations, must figure into the decision along with design features. For instance, a low-pitched roof may not be advantageous in regions of heavy snowfall, but would be in areas of extreme cold. Obviously a cabin with a loft requires a steep-pitched roof but, with wood heat, a loft may not be desirable because of the extra cords of wood needed to heat the cabin to floor level.

Building gables seems to mystify some folks, mostly due to confusion over terminology, but with an understanding of a few basic concepts, the mystery fades quickly. For our example, we'll develop a plan for a 1/4-pitch roof for a 16-foot-by-18-foot cabin and go through the steps of log construction. (The 1/4-pitch roof seems to be an excellent all-around choice, steep enough to support a hefty snow load and shed rain, but not so steep as to create needless hard-to-heat interior overhead space.) We'll plan the gables supporting two purlins and one ridgepole. On cabins larger than our example, or for looks, the plan can easily be altered to include four purlins, two on either side of the ridgepole.

Pitch indicates the incline of the roof expressed as a ratio of the vertical rise to the span. For example, if the total rise of the roof is 4 feet and the span is 16 feet, the pitch is 1/4. Simply stated then, a 1/4-pitch roof rises to a height equal to 1/4 of the span. Whether working with log or frame, the fundamentals remain the same. Carpenters as well as logsmiths speak of 1/4-, 1/3-, and 1/2-pitch roofs. The reference is to steepness; the larger the fraction, the steeper the roof. A 1/2-pitch roof, for instance, on a 16-foot-by-18-foot cabin would be very steep: 8 feet at the apex.

Don't be confused by slope. Many builders figure the incline of a roof by slope. You'll hear of slopes as 4 in 12, 6 in 12, 10 in 12. These figures simply indicate the incline of the roof in a different manner. Slope indicates the incline as a ratio of the vertical rise to the horizontal run, properly expressed as X inches in 12 inches. For example, a roof that rises 6 inches for each foot of run has a 6 in 12 slope. Our 1/4-pitch roof has a slope of 6 in 12.

You can figure incline however you like, but by the pitch seems most simple and possibly best for a first-time builder (see Figure 33).

Gables

The front dormer adds a lot to the uniqueness of the design of logsmith Philemon Morris's cedar log house in Homer. These are frame gables. The logs were imported from the Lower 48. The home has a complete block basement on a sturdy concrete foundation.

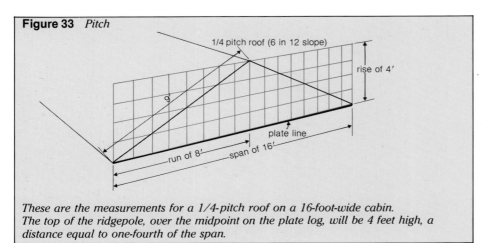

Figure 33 *Pitch*

1/4 pitch roof (6 in 12 slope)

rise of 4'

9'

plate line

run of 8' span of 16'

These are the measurements for a 1/4-pitch roof on a 16-foot-wide cabin. The top of the ridgepole, over the midpoint on the plate log, will be 4 feet high, a distance equal to one-fourth of the span.

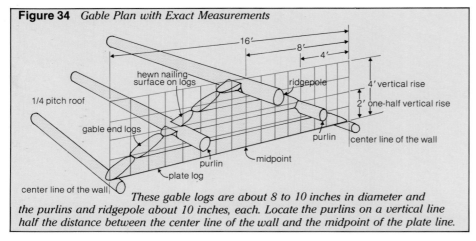

Figure 34 *Gable Plan with Exact Measurements*

16'

8'

4'

hewn nailing surface on logs

ridgepole

4' vertical rise

2' one-half vertical rise

1/4 pitch roof

gable end logs

purlin

center line of the wall

purlin

midpoint

plate log

center line of the wall

These gable logs are about 8 to 10 inches in diameter and the purlins and ridgepole about 10 inches, each. Locate the purlins on a vertical line half the distance between the center line of the wall and the midpoint of the plate line.

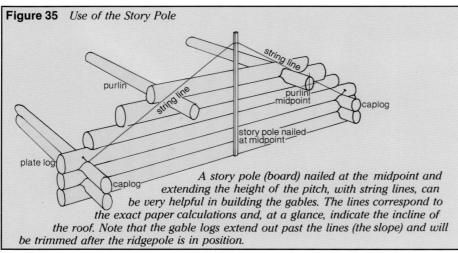

Figure 35 *Use of the Story Pole*

string line

purlin

string line

purlin midpoint

caplog

story pole nailed at midpoint

plate log

caplog

A story pole (board) nailed at the midpoint and extending the height of the pitch, with string lines, can be very helpful in building the gables. The lines correspond to the exact paper calculations and, at a glance, indicate the incline of the roof. Note that the gable logs extend out past the lines (the slope) and will be trimmed after the ridgepole is in position.

Accurately plan the gables on paper before beginning. Decide the pitch and draw a diagram of the gables to scale. Locate the position of purlins and ridgepole, calculating the actual measurements (Figure 34).

To minimize scarring and damage, always leave the gable logs, purlins, and ridgepole protected right up until the last minute. Do a superior job of cleaning and handling; you may end up looking at these logs for a lifetime.

The first log on the gable end is the plate log, notched, insulated, and pinned over the caplogs. The plate line corresponds to the bottom line of the plate log and extends through the midline of each wall, usually, but not always exactly, corresponding to the midpoint of the caplog.

To simplify actual construction, nail an upright board, called a story pole, to the midpoint of the plate line. The story pole should extend from the plate line to the actual roof height. Extend string lines from the top of the board to the top of the caplogs (Figure 35).

Make sure the lines are accurately placed. These string lines, representing the actual incline of the roof, will prove very helpful, saving repetitive calculations, with progress checked at a glance. (Note: If you are planning for exposed roof rafters, the string lines must be attached differently. Here we are planning gables with the intention of nailing tongue-and-groove decking, boards, or plywood directly to the gables, purlins, and ridgepole before the rafters are placed.)

Next, alternating butt ends, fit and pin lengths of logs up to the measured height of the midpoint of the purlins. Leave the gable logs longer than needed. The actual incline will be cut last. (Leaving the gable logs long, in stair-step fashion, proves very helpful when lifting the purlins and ridgepole onto the gables.) It's best to work on both gable ends at the same time, working to equal heights as you go.

Put the purlins up on the building, removing the string lines if necessary, but being careful to replace them exactly as they were. (On small cabins, the come-along can be used to hoist the purlins and ridgepole onto the gables,

When Brian Forbes built this cabin at
Tern Lake, he could build the gables on
the ground more easily than on the wall.
He assembled the gables with the aid
of string lines and a story pole, then
reassembled the gables on the building.
Note the inside supports for the gables,
and that the purlins and caplogs are set
at the correct pitch.

Scribe-fit cabin by Derek Stonorov. This building is complete except that the gables have not been cut at the proper pitch nor have the window or door openings been made. The gable pitch can be cut at this time. By leaving the gable logs long as the work proceeds, the purlins and ridgepole can be more easily emplaced than if an attempt had been made to trim the gable logs shorter. The most accurate way to cut the gables is with a mill attachment.

out on large log homes or structures, a gin pole or power hoist will be needed.) Use the string lines to help locate the position of the purlins. Notch them into place. Always notch the gable logs, forming a cradle for the purlins and ridgepole to sit in. *Don't* cut into purlins or the ridgepole. Correctly located, the outside edge of the purlins should contact the string lines. Before notching, don't forget to set the purlins with the proper front and back overhang. Before hoisting roof support logs, don't forget to hew or mill bearing surfaces on them so that the roof boards can be nailed down flat and even. The string lines will simplify setting the logs at the proper angle.

Next, notch a gable log over the purlins and continue building upward to ridgepole midline height. Measure down on the story pole for reference. Remove the string lines. Place the ridgepole on the gables. Notch the ridgepole into position with its top at the correct height (4 feet above the plate line on our sample).

Take extra care when notching in the ridgepole and purlins, striving for a tight, neat fit. These notches most often display the builder's skills, usually attracting much attention. Also, because heat loss here can be extreme, thoroughly insulate around the purlins and ridgepole.

Last, notch the final length of gable log over the ridgepole. Depending on the angle of the roof and the depth to which the ridgepole is notched into the lower supporting log, this log may not be needed.

Now drive a nail in at the top of the ridgepole, just in front of the gable logs. Attach the chalkbox and extend the chalkline to the top of the right caplog. Pull the line taut and snap it. Repeat the process to the left caplog. These chalklines mark the slope of the roof. Mark both gables, inside and out, the same way (Figure 36).

Using the chalklines for reference, the roof line can be cut using a chainsaw or crosscut saw. Don't attempt to cut the slope with the chainsaw held freehand at an angle. Unless supported by a mill attachment and guide, a chainsaw held at an angle

The last wall log is in place with the log milled at the correct pitch; in this case, at a 9-in-12 slope; logwork by me.

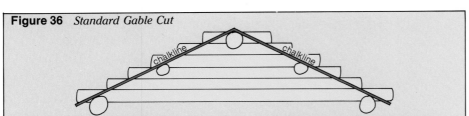

Figure 36 *Standard Gable Cut*

Chalklines mark the incline of the roof. Gable logs are left long and are helpful when setting the purlins and ridgepole on the cabin. The chalklines mark the gable cut when the decking or the roof boards are to be nailed directly to the gables, purlins, and ridgepole. The rafters then will go on top of the roof decking or boards. Note that the bearing surface is milled into the caplogs, etc.

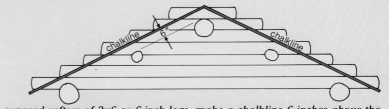

Figure 37 *Turning the Gable into a Rafter*

For exposed rafters of 2x6 or 6-inch logs, make a chalkline 6 inches above the ridgepole, purlins, and caplogs to mark the cut. (The red lines indicate the usual cut.) The gable logs must be left extra long when planning this cut. The larger the exposed rafter, the longer the gable logs must be to accommodate the higher cut.

Crude but effective supports for purlins and ridgepole where they extend out over the porch.

This is a better way to support the front extension of the ridgepole and purlins. Logwork on the Byers Lake cabin was done by Dave Johnston, Pete Robinson, and George Menard.

will tend to cut downward, resulting in an imperfect, uneven cut. You can make cuts down to the chalklines, in the same manner as sills and notches, smoothing out the slope with the saw, ax, or adz. The most precise slopes are cut with a chainsaw and mill attachment following a guide board. The Haddon Lumber/ Maker works well here.

If you are planning exposed rafters, the gables must be marked at a different height than described. For example, if the plans call for exposed 2x6s or 6-inch log rafters, the gables must be cut 6 inches higher than the slope from ridgepole to caplog (Figure 37). This higher line turns the gable end into a rafter as well. The cut must be made as high as the intended exposed rafters. In any case, make sure the gable logs are left long enough for the extra-high cut. Figures 36 and 37 show the two cuts.

You will note that it is possible to prefabricate the gables. Many builders construct the gables on the cabin, working from a high scaffold. At best this can be awkward and sometimes dangerous. On occasion, logsmiths build the gables on the ground, then reassemble them on the building. I've worked both ways. With plenty of flat ground near the cabin, and extra logs available as a base to work from, I prefer prefabrication.

First I put the plate logs on the cabin, notching them over the caplogs. Then I remove them and the caplogs, reassembling them on a squared and leveled base of supporting logs. After that I build up the gables just as if working on the cabin walls. Obviously the gable logs aren't pinned or insulated until later. The finished gables are then marked and dismantled for reassembly on the cabin. The incline is not cut until the gables are completely assembled on the wall. Some logsmiths cut the incline on the ground. This ground-level assembly makes gable construction quite simple and easy, especially when lining up the bearing surfaces of the caplogs, purlins, and ridgepole.

I've found it safer to do the gables this way. Also, it's much easier to do an accurate, clean job of cutting the incline. Although this method requires

some thought, it should not present insurmountable difficulties for the novice.

Gables can also be built of dimensional lumber instead of logs. Quick and easy, frame gables found much favor with the sourdoughs, and still prove popular with some builders. Because constructing frame gables employs more or less simple and conventional carpentry, I won't go into

much detail here, except to say that the same fundamental calculations apply to both frame and log gables. When using dimensional lumber, it's easy to measure, cut, and lay out the gable frame on the ground prior to assembly on the cabin. If desired, the frame can be strengthened to support purlins and a ridgepole. Usually the gables are boarded over with finished or rough-cut lumber or peeled slabs (Figure 38).

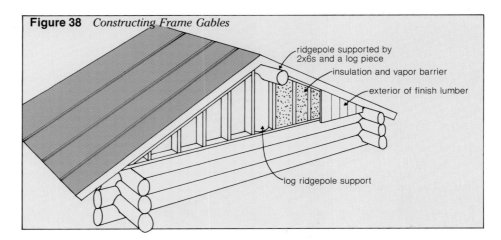

Figure 38 *Constructing Frame Gables*

ridgepole supported by 2x6s and a log piece

insulation and vapor barrier

exterior of finish lumber

log ridgepole support

These frame gables are on Kent Aslett's home. He milled the interior boards of local cottonwood, which show little sign of cracking due to a good drying period before being finished.

With the logwork nearly finished, and maybe winter close at hand, you'll be anxious to get the roof on and the logs finally under protection. This last major construction effort is also the most important. Although you may be tempted to rush to get the project closed in, don't. Take your time and do it right.

A good roof protects a cabin and contents from the elements and should offer some degree of fire resistance, which is especially important in forested areas. A quality roof is durable, requires little maintenance, and contributes to the overall appeal of the logwork. A good one is important on any building, but doubly so for a log structure. Moisture quickly ravages logs and untreated wood. Log walls, unlike frame, won't be protected with aluminum siding or latex paint. The roof must offer all necessary protection.

In Europe and in parts of Alaska, the

Curt Beddingfield built this home on Cook Inlet. The building is protected from the elements by steep roofing.

best roofs for log structures have huge overhangs that cover all of the logwork. Not only do the eaves protect from downpours, but wind-driven snow and rain as well. Quite commonly, cabins are built with ends of wall logs, purlins, or ridgepole extending out beyond the roof line. That's not good; it is a design fault with serious ramifications. Look closely at some of those protruding ends. They'll be weathered gray or black, showing water damage on the upper surfaces where moisture accumulates. Trace the logs back under the roof; you may be surprised at what you find. Oftentimes water runs along the top of the projection and under the roof line, causing any number of problems, certainly not limited to rot, but leakage as well. Even under otherwise sound roofs, I've seen ridgepoles and purlins rotted out because water drained in along the protruding logs. For a long-lasting, problem-free log structure, no portion of the logwork should be left exposed to the elements.

The very worst kind of roof to put on a log cabin is one with a covering of sod. The sod absorbs and holds moisture, and because it is a living, growing plant community, roots may

10

The Roof

This building in Wiseman dates from pre-1920. The roofing is actually old, rectangular gas cans flattened and used as shingles to protect the original pole roof. Note mud or plaster chinking between the logs.

Harold Eastwood built this beautiful cabin
in an attempt to build in an authentic
style. The fact is, however, he built better
than the vast majority of sourdough and
pioneer builders. Note the pegs holding
the eave poles in place and that the
eaves protect a stack of sized firewood.
The sod covering is mostly lichen and
moss, with a few low-growing shrubs, so
that weight is not a factor. Some sod
roofs are enormous burdens for the roof
poles to sustain for long. The sod also
absorbs and holds water that eventually
allows moisture entry to the roof when
the plants violate the underlayment.

grow down into the roof boards, allowing water in, hastening decay. Besides moisture damage, a sod roof can be quite heavy, causing undue stress. The sod for a 20-foot-by-24-foot roof can weigh 38,000 pounds, or more!

Speak of sod and most folks picture a beautiful grass-covered roof, looking much like a lawn. Although some of the better ones are just grass, many others are mini-boreal forests of grass, birch, spruce, and willow. Such plants, especially willow, quickly violate the integrity of any underlying waterproofing, with removal of the entire sod roof being the only salvation for the structure. The best sod roof I ever saw was one placed by Harold Eastwood on his remote cabin in Central Alaska. The covering was mostly lichen, a lightweight and long-growing plant. The insulative value of the covering might be questionable, but the weight and moisture retention capabilities of the plants are not.

Stampeders, prospectors, and other pioneers used sod as insulation. They'd put the logs up fast, roof the cabin with boards or spruce poles, up to 200 per cabin, throw down tar paper or cardboard, if they had any, and then pile on the sod. With this built-in, self-destruct system, their cabins didn't last long. We might call them the first biodegradable form of housing.

A sod roof, as might be expected, can also be very flammable, especially in the fall and summer when they are bare of snow and the dry grasses and leaves are exposed.

The best roof to put on a log building is fire- and weather-resistant and maintenance-free. That means metal, and metal roofs are expensive. Recently I worked on a 28-foot-by-36-foot cabin and the owner opted for steel roofing. When complete, including the decking, insulation, roofing, and labor, the roof alone cost him $9,500 (1998 price). But after all the hard work and care that went into that project, that expenditure ensured a long life for his log home.

Roll roofing or asphalt shingles cost less than aluminum or steel sheets, but in the long run, the extra maintenance and repairs needed for these second-choice coverings will surpass the

Kim Blair and Bill Kisken set the roof support truss on the Northern Lights Gift Shop at Denali Park. These two builders are at the top of their craft.

initial difference in cost and, over time, end up being more expensive.

Let's close in a cabin with a standard roof (Figure 40). Actually there's no such thing as a standard roof—every builder seems to have a unique style—but our standard roof is more common than others.

After the logwork is completed, with the ridgepole and purlins set in place and the slope of the gable ends cut,

we're ready to begin. First, nail decking, boards, or plywood at right angles to the ridgepole and across the caplogs, extending them out over the walls a suitable distance to form the desired overhang. Cover the entire building; 2x6 tongue-and-groove decking is the preferred covering since it's stout enough to be self-supporting. (A 4-foot overhang is not too much, but most likely anything greater than that may

need external support to keep the eaves from sagging.) The front and rear projections are determined by the length of the caplogs, purlins, and ridgepole. A 4-foot overhang on three sides and a 6-foot front overhang is ideal.

On a small cabin with a conventional roof, a truss-support system is unnecessary, but if you have your heart set on a sod roof, such a roof—on any size cabin—should be supported with trusses (Figure 39). Large log buildings and smaller ones with low-pitched roofs in areas of heavy snowfall also need truss support. A scissor, or king post, truss works well. On buildings with a tie log, vertical uprights from the tie log to the purlins and ridgepole may suffice.

Next, cut out all the plumbing vent, electrical, or chimney openings. It's best not to have any more openings than absolutely necessary. Perhaps all you'll need is a chimney hole.

The best roofs have R-40 or greater insulation, with appropriate ventilation to carry away moisture; plywood sheathing over the rafters for strength; and a tar-paper covering under the steel metal roofing.

In Alaska and other northern climes, a couple of special roof design features are important. To minimize condensation damage to the ceiling and ice buildup on the eaves, the roof cavity must be kept cool and free of moisture by a combination of adequate vapor barrier and proper ventilation. Louvers and eave slots provide the cross ventilation. Cover the roof boards with 4- to 6-mil plastic sheeting, preferably in one piece. Be sure to seal the plastic around all the openings through the roof. Ideally, the one-piece vapor barrier will keep out all moisture.

After enclosing the building with the decking or boards and covering them with a one-piece vapor barrier, and then cutting out the openings, build the rafter system and chimney support frame. Use oversize rafters since good ventilation space will be left above the insulation level without any additional effort. The rafters can be placed on 2-foot or 4-foot centers, depending on your roof design and intended insulation. If you plan on using fiberglass in rolls, or 2-foot sheets of insulfoam, the rafters

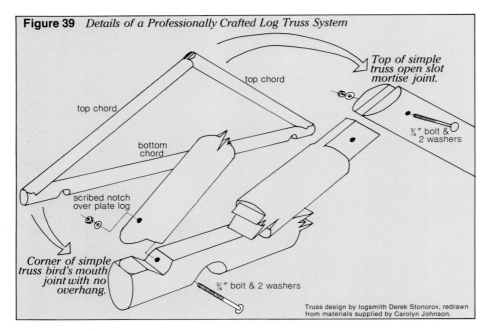

Figure 39 *Details of a Professionally Crafted Log Truss System*

top chord

top chord

Top of simple truss open slot mortise joint.

bottom chord

¾" bolt & 2 washers

scribed notch over plate log

Corner of simple truss bird's mouth joint with no overhang.

¾" bolt & 2 washers

Truss design by logsmith Derek Stonorov, redrawn from materials supplied by Carolyn Johnson.

Single post truss on a sauna by Dave Johnston; note the bird's-mouth cut at left.

Metal roofing comes in many colors, and this red-colored steel roof on the home of Jean Romig, in Cooper Landing, greatly enhances its beauty. The house was built by Paul Smith, with two-sided logs.

Dave Johnston, Pete Robinson, and George Menard used dead-standing timber to build the Byers Lake cabin. It took 25 poles to cover just one side of the porch. The exterior is covered with aluminum press sheets, obtained cheaply from a newspaper, then with heavy plastic sheeting, and then with sod.

A half-pole roof on a small cabin. Instead of using whole poles, the builder split the poles lengthwise to cover the roof. The poles were first split with a chainsaw, then the two halves were laid side by side, face up. A saw was run between them several times until a relatively close fit along their length was achieved. The adjoining half-logs were fit the same way.

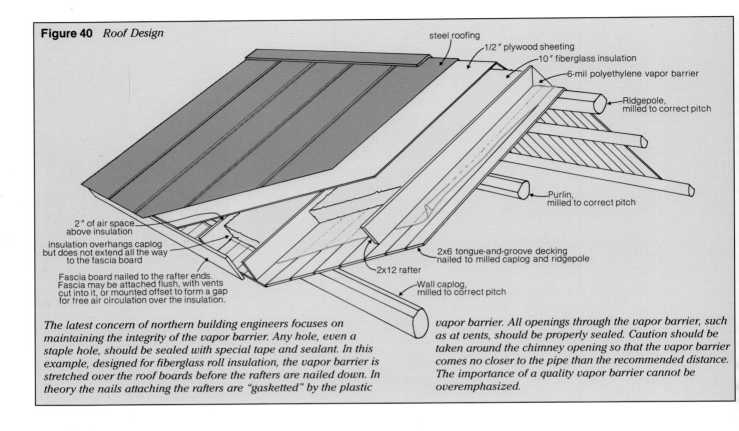

Figure 40 *Roof Design*

steel roofing

1/2″ plywood sheeting

10″ fiberglass insulation

6-mil polyethylene vapor barrier

Ridgepole, milled to correct pitch

Purlin, milled to correct pitch

2x6 tongue-and-groove decking nailed to milled caplog and ridgepole

2x12 rafter

Wall caplog, milled to correct pitch

2″ of air space above insulation

insulation overhangs caplog but does not extend all the way to the fascia board

Fascia board nailed to the rafter ends. Fascia may be attached flush, with vents cut into it, or mounted offset to form a gap for free air circulation over the insulation.

The latest concern of northern building engineers focuses on maintaining the integrity of the vapor barrier. Any hole, even a staple hole, should be sealed with special tape and sealant. In this example, designed for fiberglass roll insulation, the vapor barrier is stretched over the roof boards before the rafters are nailed down. In theory the nails attaching the rafters are "gasketted" by the plastic vapor barrier. All openings through the vapor barrier, such as at vents, should be properly sealed. Caution should be taken around the chimney opening so that the vapor barrier comes no closer to the pipe than the recommended distance. The importance of a quality vapor barrier cannot be overemphasized.

This 8-inch milled-log cabin built by Frank Entsminger in North Pole has a pole roof that is rather steep. Usually pole roofs go on low-pitched roofs. Note how Frank jogged the roof line to allow for light and visibility for windows.

should be on 2-foot centers. Depending on design, some builders place rafters on 16-inch centers.

Build a louvered vent in the rafters at each end above the gables. Cut slots, or drill holes in the eaves, above the insulation for required cross ventilation. Screen over all openings to keep out squirrels and other pests. Next, install your insulation. No matter what type of insulation you intend to use, the minimum recommended R-value (R stands for resistance to heat loss; the higher the R-number, the better the insulation) for ceilings in northern homes, according to the University of Alaska Extension Service, is R-40. The Canadian Electrical Association recommends R-40 as minimum. Because it keeps the insulation dry, a quality vapor barrier allows the insulation's full potential to be realized. The insulation also should overhang the walls 8 to 12 inches. In winter, it may be -40°, or colder, on the outside, and you'll be trying to maintain 70° inside; since warm air rises, it is easier and cheaper to heat a cabin if the roof is insulated correctly.

After the insulation is in place and the flashing has been placed around the vents and chimney openings, attach the nailers to the rafters. Finally, apply the roofing material. (If you opt for a complete plywood covering, then the flashing will go on after the plywood.)

Since roofing is basic conventional carpentry, I'll not go into any more detail. The one feature peculiar to building a roof on a log house is the method used to nail the roof boards to the logs. If you merely nail boards across from the ridgepole to the caplogs, and at the center to the purlins, the logs may not settle correctly. Remember: The log builder must always plan for and cope with settling. Though it's not universal among logsmiths, many professionals slot the roof boards before nailing them to the purlins and caplogs. You can nail to the ridgepole without slotting the boards. But at the purlins and caplogs, an electric power saw cut about 4 or 5 inches long should be made for each nail. During settling, the slots allow the roof boards to move or float unimpeded as the logs settle.

Building with exposed rafters is quite uncommon in Alaska. Rarely do you see a new log building constructed with exposed log rafters, mainly because it entails the construction of two sets of rafters, one for view, and one above the ceiling to support the roofing and make space for the insulation. However, one Southeast Alaska logsmith builds cabins with false rafters made of logs. Though merely cosmetic, the false rafters look good and add a sense of strength and stoutness to his buildings.

Choice of roofing materials will be influenced by initial cost, durability, maintenance cost, and appearance. Slope also limits the selection; low roofs require a more watertight covering than steep roofs.

Probably the best roofing material is treated steel, called Terne metal roofing. Not only does treated steel resist weather better than most other types of

King post truss over a porch of a Tom Corr–built log home.

This lovely log home near Delta has a cedar shingle roof. Shingles or shakes look beautiful and blend naturally with the surroundings, but they are not a good idea in areas of potential wildfire hazard.

roofing, it's also fire-resistant. Terne metal is available in 4-foot-wide sheets, up to 16 feet long (longer in some areas), and comes in earth-tone colors: brown, red, and green.

Aluminum is also a quality choice, although it is not as durable as steel. Limbs, cones, and such are always blowing down on a roof, and I've seen some aluminum coverings quite badly damaged by wind-driven tree limbs. Aluminum is as easy to use as steel and comes in a variety of designs, lengths, and widths. Metal roofing of either kind should be used on a roof with a slope of less than 3 in 12, because of the possibility of ice buildup on the eaves.

Asphalt roofing comes three ways: as saturated felts, as mineral surface in rolls, and as mineral-surface shingles. The felts, in varying weights, are best used as the underlayment, but they have been used extensively in bush areas as the primary roofing, though usually with poor results. The main drawback to these roofing materials is their lack of durability: All are easily damaged and have high maintenance needs. Repairs to asphalt roofs require an application of tar, sometimes after each rainstorm.

In all fairness (my obvious bias toward metal showing) mineral-coat shingles, properly applied, are quite satisfactory. Mineral-fiber shingles, also called cement shingles, are also an extremely good-quality roofing. Before the advent of treated metal, all types of asphalt roofing were used throughout Alaska with varying results. Probably tar-paper roofing and flattened gas cans (Blazo shingles) were the two most common roofing materials in bush Alaska.

Most experts agree that wood shingles should not be applied to slopes of less than 4 in 12, and many log builders claim less than 6 in 12. According to the University of Alaska Extension Service, wood shingles should

never be used in extremely cold regions because of glaciering. However, if they are used, a 45-pound felt roll-roofing underlayment is advised to minimize leaks caused by glaciering. One must admit that nothing looks more beautiful or harmonious in a natural setting than a log home topped with wood shingles. Many folks using a froe (or frow), a special tool used to cut shingles from a log round, make their own shakes, as hand-split shingles are called. Cedar is the preferred wood, but shakes are made from any straight-grained wood.

Another serious concern with wood-shingle roofs is the susceptibility to fire. Many underwriters will not insure a home with a combustible roof in areas of high fire potential, except as a high risk, which means stiff premiums. Shingle roofs should not be used in areas with a history of brush or forest fires. Hot sparks from stovepipes have also started shingle roofs ablaze. Steel or aluminum should be the preferred material in high fire danger areas.

Always use the best-quality stovepipe assembly and roof jack available—meaning insulated pipe and attachments. Chimney fires are a real hazard and there's no need burning down a good log home because of faulty or uninsulated pipe.

No matter what your roofing choice, seal around the chimney opening and plumbing vents. A drip edge to protect the eaves is a good idea, and use flashing where necessary. Do everything you can to make the roof as watertight and as maintenance-free as possible. If you're not sure, seek professional advice or help.

As a final measure, put rain gutters with downspouts around your building. Not only can you collect water for daily use, but a full rain barrel is also a proven fire-fighting aid. Too, the gutters will help protect the bottom logs from the splash of rain where it pours off the roof.

Take a deep breath and relax. The roof's on. There's still lots to do, but bad weather can hit and you can work under protection.

The next step is to close in the building completely, installing windows and doors. First, though, get out the chainsaw a last time and do all the final trim work. If you waited till you got the roof on to cut to size all the windows and door openings, do that now and spline the openings. Also cut the chamfers at the openings and trim the log ends.

If the weather's good and you're in no hurry to move in, clean and prepare the logs for an application of preservative and finish. Soap and water, plus bleach, will remove all the boot marks, mold, dirt, and stains that accumulated during construction. Sand any damaged or rough places where chains, cables, or peavey hooks scarred the logs. After a thorough cleaning and dusting, the logs are ready for the application of a protective finish.

Some logsmiths don't wait this long to apply preservative to the logs, but make applications as they go. Logs can mildew and stain on the wall as easily as on the ground. One logsmith uses a hand-sprayer, the large weed-killer type applicator, to apply a coat of a powerful fungicide and insecticide to the logs as soon as they are peeled. Not only does this protect them from insects and moisture, but from staining as well. Thoroughly review options. Some preservatives have harmful ingredients that may impact the inhabitants of the building. A few products are highly poisonous and should be applied with care: Avoid skin contact, inhalation, or accidental ingestion. (A man I know killed all of the plants

Finishing Up

Builder Darwin Seim created this unique home on Chena Ridge Road near Fairbanks.

Brian Forbes touches up the logs with a sander-grinder before bleaching and cleaning the logs. Note the plug-in that has been recessed into the logs.

in his greenhouse merely by coating the exposed wood studs with an old-style wood preservative containing pentachlorophenol (penta). Never use highly toxic wood finishes on interior surfaces, especially in kitchens, bedrooms, and bathrooms. "Sick buildings" result from the release of chemical toxins found in some floor coverings, wood finishes, and insulations.

All manner of wood preservatives and finishes have been used on logs: varnish, shellac, tung oil, Danish oil, linseed oil, shingle oil, logwood oil, Varathane, clear plastic, Rawhide, sanding sealer, and floor hardener. Each has its advantages and disadvantages. Perhaps the best way is to apply a primary coat of sanding sealer, followed by your choice of finish.

Exterior surfaces can be protected from the ravages of insects, moisture, and ultraviolet (UV) light with three-coat, hard finishes. Interior surfaces can be protected with water-based or oil finishes. Some of these interior finishes are non-yellowing, non-flammable, non-toxic, and odorless. LIFELINE, by Perma-Chink, is one example.

In the final analysis, the finish chosen depends in part on local conditions. In areas of wind-driven snow and rain, a product such as Rawhide is preferable to an oil finish. Also, in areas with dust storms or along dirt roads, oil finishes are not good because dust will stick and settle on the logs. On the other hand, a logwood oil finish is an excellent choice in sheltered areas.

No matter what finish you apply, the logs are going to check or crack; even the dry ones will. I once used a fire-killed log, dead 10 years, that I felt had to be at the minimum moisture content level of 15%, and it still cracked. Don't think of the checking as blemishes that have to be filled or hidden, but, rather, as the natural state of logs. The checking adds character.

In the end, try to use a finish that enhances the natural appeal of logs. No matter what you use, apply the preservative on a calm day, and do the inside and outside all at the same time.

Allow plenty of drying time before working again on the building.

When preparing the logs for finishing, you might also pound ship's rope oakum into the cracks between two-sided or round logs, or apply a thin line of caulking. In the old days, mud or clay was used to seal the cracks between logs. Today, synthetic caulks (silicone, butyls, or other types) offer ease of application and superior quality, hardening to springy toughness. Use a caulk gun to apply material and do as neat a job as possible.

Somehow it seems a shame to buy a factory door and put it on an honest log building. There's no great secret to it, so go ahead and build your own door. I've seen many fine doors made from home-milled boards, slabs of logs, and full round logs. Each, built neatly and cleanly, looked good. I like to use 2x6 decking, usually building the door from the scraps left over from the roof. A Z-design bolted across the boards holds the whole thing together. It can be a single thickness of 2x6s, or a layered affair with insulation between the layers. If your cabin has an arctic entry, you need only single-thickness doors. Without an entryway, you'd best build an insulated door, especially if you heat solely with wood.

Black bolts and hinges add an ornamental look to a handcrafted door. You can use standard strap or butt hinges, or make elaborate ones. Some craftsmen whittle hinges from wood, topping off the door with a wooden latch as well.

One of the most costly items in any building can be the windows. Quality windows are very expensive. Good ones seal in heat, keep out the cold, and open for ventilation. In Alaska, double-pane windows should be considered minimum, and triple panes are best. You can spend a small fortune on such windows, perhaps an amount equal to the cost of all the rest of the materials used in the cabin. To save real money, make your own windows. Have a glass company seal together double or triple panes, and then you build the sash. Windows don't have to be the fancy crank-open kind. A simple frame will do, then you can put hinges on the frame

The spruce door and handle on the cabin at Byers Lake; note the chamfer at the door opening. Four stout strap hinges support the door. Logwork by Dave Johnston, Pete Robinson, and George Menard.

Beautiful slab door built by Roger Cline for a Homer cabin.

A simple door on a Tern Lake cabin; logwork by Brian Forbes.

Gerry Norris built this door for the kitchen area of the O. G. Simpson home near Bean Creek; logwork by Dick Quinn.

and open the windows as you would the door. Old-fashioned windows, like barn sash, are much cheaper than are the modern designs. You can also scrounge old windows and rehabilitate them for use in your cabin. One cabin I worked on had windows salvaged from an old hospital. The owner sanded the frames, reglazed them, and installed them in the cabin. Nine windows, total cost $125. Not bad.

A small cabin, like our 16-foot-by-18-foot example, should have four windows, one on each wall. The side windows, over the dining area, work area, or kitchen sink, should be quite large to allow in adequate natural light. The front and rear windows can be smaller, but should open to allow for ample cross-ventilation. If you make your own picture windows for the side walls, you might even save enough to buy the fancy crank-open windows for front and back.

Don't be tempted to fit the door and windows flush in the openings. Leave the required settling space above each. Stuff the openings with insulation. If you don't want to look at the gaps until the logs finish settling, and as a measure to keep out squirrels and such, nail a trim board to the frames to hide the gaps. Don't nail to the logs, since those nails would affect the settling; nail to the frame instead.

With the doors and windows in and the finish applied to the logs, it's time to think about partitions.

You probably won't need a partition in a small cabin, though you might want to section the room off. In larger cabins and homes, partitions are almost required for the best use of the space. Finish the partitions in a natural wood such as knotty pine or clear spruce that will reflect the light and keep the interior from becoming too dark.

Any partition must be designed so that it will not interfere with settling of the logs. If you fit a partition tightly to the space below a tie log, you might be surprised one day to come home and find the partition shattered or twisted completely out of place. More likely the partition will hold the tie log up, prevent proper settling, and cause gaps to form between the logs. Also, never nail an

Railing in the Northern Lights Gift Shop at Denali Park. Kim Blair's handiwork.

Simple framing of log slabs highlights this window in the home built by Bill and Nanci Arpino in Tok.

Instead of using conventional 2x material to frame the windows in this house, the carpenter used 4x material, which adds a feeling of strength and stoutness to the framing and blends nicely with the logs.

This interesting window trim is on the Fairbanks Visitors Center, which was built by Harold Herning. Note the caulking and hard, clear finish on the two-sided logs.

To the right of this window in the Byers Lake cabin is a deep mortise in the logs that allows the window to slide open—the glass slides into the wall and out again. Note the natural slab window trim and how the burl has been scribe-fit to the log below.

upright, like the studs in a partition, to a log wall. The nails, too, will hold the logs apart and cause uneven settling. Everything you put in a cabin must be planned to allow for the natural settling of the logs. Leave space above partitions, and wherever you must nail uprights to the wall, cut vertical slots, as you did for the roof boards, for the nails to slide in.

About Stoves for Cabins

A wood stove might be your only source of heat, or just an auxiliary. As late as 1940, wood was the main source of heat for about one out of every four homes in the United States. By 1970, however, wood heated only about 2% of all U.S. homes. Then came the energy shortage of the 1970s and the higher costs of home heating fuels. In the early 1970s fewer than 200,000 wood stoves were sold annually in the United States; by the end of the decade, a million stoves a year were being sold.

You need to think about several things when purchasing a stove, such as: Is the stove too big or too small to heat the requisite space? How effective will it be in providing heat? Will it hold a fire overnight? How well made is it? How safe is it?

Good stoves are airtight, providing only enough air to sustain the fire, which allows the fuel to last longer and surrender more heat. Positive air control is also positive fire control. An airtight stove will also hold a fire overnight and have enough coals left in the morning to refire with just a stoking. Poor-quality stoves leak air and burn fuel inefficiently, and are dangerous. Poor stoves will sometimes allow the fire to flare up, despite the dampers and controls being closed. At best, poor stoves are only about 40% efficient, pouring 60% of their heat up the chimney. Good airtight stoves deliver 60% efficiency. Quality wood stoves are built to exacting standards. Most have a secondary combustion chamber, brick lining, and foolproof locking door.

Probably one of the most Alaskan of all stoves is the old standard barrel stove. Since these creations hold a lot of wood, they'll heat a large area. Actually, though,

Fire is always a hazard. Note the rock "safe," Chimgard, and fire extinguisher near the woodstove in Therese Norris's home.

113

they use fuel quite inefficiently and are subject to burnout, thus making them not completely reliable. Most are home-built by fitting kits to 55-gallon drums. Barrel stoves heat cabins and homes from Barrow to Ketchikan.

In my opinion, Vermont Castings, Blaze King, the Earth Stove, and the Fisher Mama Bear (Baby Bear in small quarters) are the best stoves available.

Above all else your stove must be safe. Cabin fires, unfortunately, are so common in Alaska as to almost be part of the northern experience. This need not be so.

Install the stove properly. Experts recommend that wood stoves be a minimum of 24 inches from unprotected logs. Set your stove on a noncombustible floor covering; insulated sheeting is the best choice, although safes made of dirt, tiles, rock, and brick also work well. The floor covering should be 12 inches wider on each side than the stove and 18 inches longer in front. Always use quality stovepipe—double-insulated pipe is best—and install the pipe according to the manufacturer's recommended procedures.

Alaska fire authorities agree that most fires related to wood stove operation are not caused by the stove but, rather, are due to faulty installation and lack of maintenance to the stovepipe or chimney. Chimney fires are dreaded on cold arctic nights, and often end tragically. If a chimney fire starts and you're not prepared, there's little you can do. Just closing the stove down may not put the fire out. You'll need an extinguisher. Ever wonder why sourdoughs keep ladders up against the cabin next to the chimney? Access for cleaning the pipe or for fighting fire. One fire marshal I talked with said that the old technique of climbing on the roof and pouring water down a burning chimney was not without risk—you might slip and fall off the roof or, worse, if the roof burned out, fall into the burning building. He advised cutting off the fire at the source, in the stove, by attacking it with an A and B dry chemical extinguisher, or flare-type extinguisher. He explained that the intense draft of the fire will suck the dry chemical powder from the stove and

up the chimney. Then, after using the extinguisher, close all the dampers and doors of the stove to shut off the oxygen.

Many Alaska homesteaders keep salt handy to pour down the chimney in case of chimney fires. Most experts agree that salt doesn't do anything faster or better than plain dirt, sand, or fine gravel. Also, the residue of salt when combined with moisture will cause serious corrosion of the chimney lining, thereby creating a much greater future potential fire hazard.

A red-hot chimney, with blast-furnace-hot flames roaring out of it, will imperil any roof and chill most anyone's nerves. The pipe can melt or burn out and ignite rafters and the entire roof. When that happens it might be too late to do anything but watch. Most chimney fires seem to occur at 3:00 A.M. in mid-January with the temperature well below zero. On such an occasion, any fire fighters are hampered by the extreme cold and most cabins end up a total loss, with loss of life not uncommon. It seems so sad when most chimney fires can be avoided.

Chimney fires result when flue gas temperatures rise dangerously high and ignite creosote deposits in the pipe, stove, and fittings. Creosote is a flammable substance that condenses out of the flue gases as a hard or flaky deposit on the inside of the pipe, chimney, and stove. A buildup of only 1/4 inch of creosote can be hazardous, with severe accumulations fuel for potentially catastrophic chimney fires. Creosote builds up over time and if left unchecked can nearly close a stovepipe. When flue gases soar to 1,000° to 1,500°, which is quite possible when the stove is lighted or loaded, the creosote buildup may ignite. Clean the pipe regularly with a long-handled brush, and keep the stove within safe temperature ranges.

Because of the danger, never overfire your stove. An overfired stove may glow bright red and suffer extensive damage not easily discernible. The excess heat may crack or warp the metal, open joints, and otherwise seriously erode the integrity of the unit. You often hear people talk of having hot fires to "burn out the creosote." One day they might

ignite the stuff at an uncontrollable rate. Instead, keep the fire at tolerable levels and clean the chimney religiously. A good investment, and also an inexpensive one, is a simple flue thermometer, the type that shows operating temperature and indicates safe operating ranges by color coding. (A good, magnetic stick-on thermometer is the Chim-Gard.) A safe temperature range is 350° to 800°, with temperatures below that encouraging creosote formation. The flue thermometer not only will warn you at a glance of overfiring, but also aid you in keeping the stove at optimum temperatures. One look can warn of impending danger and corrective action can be taken before tragedy strikes.

Also, to avoid creosote buildup, always use dry and seasoned wood. Dry birch burns hot and lasts longest, and remains a choice firewood. Wet or damp woods give off excess moisture and hasten creosote formation. You'll have plenty of scraps and log ends available after cabin construction, but don't use them in the stove unless they are thoroughly dry.

There's an old sourdough saying that goes: "It's never too cold to cut wood when you're out of fire." It might be a good idea to get in a stack of firewood and let it season while you're building the cabin. Wood seasoned 12 months gives 100% fuel value, but green or unseasoned wood gives only 63% fuel value. Obviously, it takes less dry wood to heat a cabin than wet wood. With a stack of seasoned wood next to the cabin, you'll be prepared to work right up to and through snowfall. There's one major undeniable point in favor of small cabins and homes: They're easy on firewood, and any stove can retain command and keep you warm.

The question is, how warm and comfortable will the cabin actually be? This depends entirely on the size of logs you used and how well you built it. There's a lot of controversy on the comfort factor of log homes versus frame homes. Although one expert calculated the heat loss of 8-inch round logs to be twice as high as 2x4 stud frame walls with full insulation, I find that

A log cabin on a homestead near Rink Creek, Gustavus, in Southeastern Alaska. Note the ladder, rain gutters, and rain barrel. (E. A. Mills)

Home in Eagle, built in 1975 by Jack
Greene with two-sided logs. Note asphalt
roll roofing, entryway, long eaves that
provide cover for drying firewood and
protection for log ends, and the rain
gutters that direct water into barrels on
pallets. The gravel around the front door
and the walkway is a good idea, too.

The log door and latch to a
Dave Johnston–built sauna. Not a
logsmith, but a park ranger, Dave
nevertheless has an eye for detail and
love of logwork.

These distinctive windows are in the south gable end of a log home in Talkeetna built by Tom Ross. In combination, the logs framing the window join with the slanting logs to form a simple truss that supports the roof.

This is the door to the J. C. Quast home at Auke Bay, near Juneau.

Log furniture and custom-insulated door in the author's Denali Park home. The coffee table was made from a half-log left over from a window cut; the legs are diamond willow.

hard to accept. The R-value of a log is figured at 1.25 to 1.95 per each inch of thickness for seasoned logs having 12% moisture content. That's a lot of variation. Some use the lower figure to prove that log walls are not as efficient as frame walls in retaining heat, while other experts use the higher figure to indicate that logs are of greater insulative value.

The problem as I see it lies not with the logs, but the way they are used. The quality of log construction varies so much from builder to builder that blanket statements just can't be made. In general, frame buildings are warmer because most building techniques are standardized and performance standards are established, so there is little variation from building to building. There's no standardization in log construction. What constitutes quality construction to one person might be slipshod to another. Until some form of standardization is outlined, log buildings will not match up, on the average, with the heat efficiency of frame buildings, though some will be better. So, how warm and comfortable will your log home be? It will depend on how well you built.

Hopefully, this book will help you avoid many of the mistakes I fell into when starting out. When that first puff of smoke springs from your wilderness cabin or urban log home, you've got much to be proud of. Enjoy the sense of accomplishment. Ships are launched with a champagne bottle smashed across the bow. You could do the same against the point of the ridgepole. Or, better yet, sit down and drink it in celebration. You earned it.

Being a good logsmith means more than being proficient at logwork. A good logsmith needs the eye of an artist and an eclectic's view of life. Brian Forbes possesses the finest qualities of a logsmith: engineer, artist in wood, and designer par excellence. He knows that log homes are synergistic—the parts greater than their sum. Note the details in the corner of his family's onetime home: the hinges, the Dutch door, round window, the heart cut into the upright of the almost Old-World bookshelf—details that make a log house a home and more.

Part Two

In a broad sense, log structures have housed Alaskans since almost the time the first migrants crossed the Bering Sea land bridge into the New World.

Along the coast, Inupiat Eskimos and their ancestors built sod houses supported with frames of driftwood logs. The Yup'ik Eskimos of Western Alaska built their similar *barabaras* of sod and logs cut from the surrounding forests. A fine example of a *barabara* can be seen today by visitors to Brooks Camp in Katmai National Park and Preserve.

In Southeast Alaska, Natives used the wealth of cedar and spruce to build ceremonial houses, homes, and forts. Whole villages were built of massive, hewn logs for defensive, artistic, and ceremonial purposes. Some examples of their craftsmanship, including totems, are preserved to this day.

An original Yup'ik Eskimo barabara *at Brooks Camp, Katmai National Park and Preserve.* (E. A. Mills)

It's hard today to find good examples of Russian logwork, for many have been lost to fire. There's a lot of architecture of Russian influence about, but most was built after Alaska became part of the United States in 1867. In Kodiak, the Baranov Museum, listed as a National Historic Landmark under the name Erskine House, was built as a warehouse in about 1792 by the Russian-American Company. The 36-foot-by-72-foot, two-story, squared-log building is one of the oldest remaining structures of Russian origin in the state. In 1880, the Alaska Commercial Company covered the logs with siding, with another layer of siding covering that later, but inside, wall sections have been uncovered to reveal the log construction. The building originally had a wood foundation but that was replaced with stone prior to 1948, and the original Russian-style hip roof was altered to a more modern gable style.

In Kenai, at Fort Kenay, the two-story Holy Assumption of the Virgin Mary Russian Orthodox Church, built in 1895, is also a log structure joined with dovetail notches and covered with siding. Though built 30 years after the

Log History

This old log building near Copper Center, with squared saddle notches, is slowly disintegrating. The holes in the roof and between the shakes have let in the rain and snow so that most of the logs are now rotten beyond salvage. It is a shame that so much of Alaskan history crumbles into dust this way.

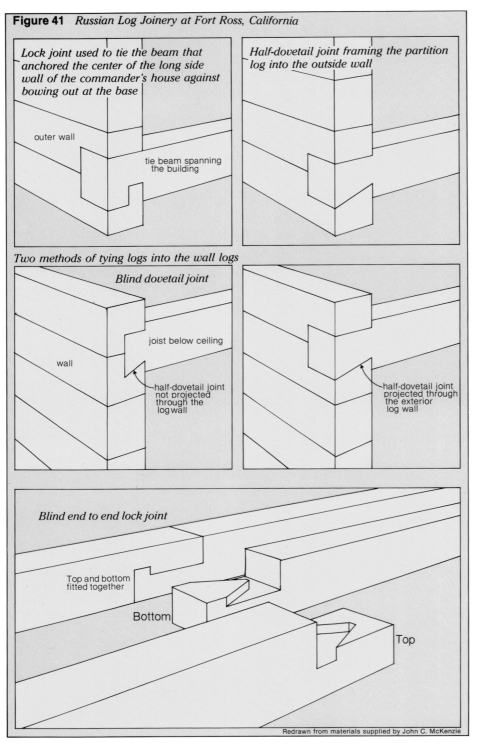

Figure 41 *Russian Log Joinery at Fort Ross, California*

Lock joint used to tie the beam that anchored the center of the long side wall of the commander's house against bowing out at the base

outer wall

tie beam spanning the building

Half-dovetail joint framing the partition log into the outside wall

Two methods of tying logs into the wall logs

Blind dovetail joint

joist below ceiling

wall

half-dovetail joint not projected through the log wall

half-dovetail joint projected through the exterior log wall

Blind end to end lock joint

Top and bottom fitted together

Bottom

Top

Redrawn from materials supplied by John C. McKenzie

Alaska Purchase, the logwork was done by Russian settlers and Kenaitze Indians in traditional style. This church is considered the best-preserved example of 19th-century Russian Orthodox Church design in Alaska.

To the north of the church stands the frame-covered log rectory built in 1868, one year after Alaska became an American possession. Nearby is the cupola-topped St. Nicholas Memorial Chapel, built between 1906 and 1911. This building, also of typical styling, is uncovered, with the logs and notches fully exposed to view—and weathering. On examination, you can see the ax marks, moss chinking, and close fit of the logs and notches. Unfortunately, this building suffers from exposure to the elements.

One other example of Russian logwork worth viewing is the blockhouse replica, built with the tenon-style corners like those of Old New Archangel, that dominates the Russian cemetery at Sitka.

The principal log building still left in Sitka from the Russian era is the Bishop's House built in 1842 by Finnish artisans. The useful life of the building began when Bishop Innocent, who later became Metropolitan of Moscow, chief among all Russian bishops, occupied the building as his residence in December 1843. He termed the two-story structure a "mansion." The logwork in the building is of exceptional quality, and the entire building has been restored by the National Park Service.

All of the log structures in both Alaska and California were built of very similar designs. The Rotchev House built at Fort Ross, California, in 1836 as the residence for the new colony manager, Alexander Rotchev, is almost identical in design to the Erskine House (Baranov Museum) in Kodiak. The joinery, though similar, is not identical. The end-to-end joints in Kodiak are all stepped to prevent horizontal separation, while in the Rotchev House all but five joints were nothing more than simple end-to-end mortise and tenon.

The original manager of Fort Ross was Ivan Kuskov, the man who developed Sitka (New Archangel) into

This Russian Orthodox memorial to Father Nicholas stands near the Holy Assumption of the Virgin Mary Russian Orthodox Church in Kenai. Built in about 1906 of hewn logs and dovetail notches, and chinked with moss, the shrine is unfurnished and sadly open to the ravages of the weather. On St. Nicholas's Day, December 19, prayers are said at an altar and icon brought from the main church. Old photos show the shrine painted white with a single blue dome. The quality workmanship is still impressive, despite the obvious decay.

prominence, so similarities in design should not be that surprising. The typical Alaska and California Russian-American Company log architecture has been termed Siberian. John C. McKenzie, who was present at the Fort Ross restoration effort in 1946–50 and active during the current restoration effort there, offered me the following description of the original construction:

While the log buildings were constructed with hewn and shaped logs up to 2 feet in diameter, larger logs were split and hewn for the steep, lap-board roofs. By careful selection some large redwood logs were split into roof boards 2 inches thick, 16 inches wide, and up to 20 feet long. These were hewn smooth, with two troughs on each about 3 inches wide and 1 inch deep chiseled down the entire length of the upper face and about an inch from the sides. These were then nailed in two overlapping layers from the eave to the peak of the roof. Steep roofs, usually hip roofs, typical.

The half-dovetail joints at the exterior corners include a drop

block which dropped into the lower log to prevent separation. It was set, however, so that water could enter on the sloping face of the half-dovetail, which would accumulate water in the mortise, eventually rotting out the corner. In Kodiak the joint was inverted and the mortise was set in an upper face of the joint.

Window and door frames are heavy, some of 8x8 timbers depending on the thickness of the adjoining wall. The side posts next to openings are grooved down the outer side to receive the tenons of the adjoining logs. Headers drop onto the vertical posts and fit with a mortise and tenon, secured in place with two opposing wedges.

Wall logs were caulked with forest moss, and were self-sealing. Outer doors appear to have been large single doors but interior ones were double with a drop pin on one door.

Metal "tie rods" were occasionally found in the top wall logs and in large tie logs that spanned the building above the central partition. These went

through the cross logs and bound the side walls together against the stress of the heavy roof. One such rod had the blacksmith's mark still visible. The four-sided rod was about 1 1/2 inches in diameter and perhaps 30 inches long, needle-pointed with a flat head.

Several hand-wrought iron nails and spikes were found. They differ from the typical American "iron cut nail" in several ways. . . . Most significantly they all seem rust-free. This was explained when an original iron ingot from the site of the original blacksmith's shop was sent to metallurgists for analysis. That ingot had been poured in "black sand," a very high gold-bearing sand, and the ingot was practically gold-plated. No wonder such nails were rust-resistant.

Steep roof; walls set into the ground; floors well above ground level; shuttered windows; large, centrally located stoves of brick used for cooking, heating, and sleeping; and ship-lapped boards used in the floor, ceiling, and all partitions are typical features of this "Siberian" construction.

This replica of a Russian blockhouse was built in 1962 by the National Park Service and stands on the exact spot of the original, overlooking Sitka. As evidenced by this close-up, the Russians built well to fend off attacks by the Tlingits. In 1802 the Tlingits did attack and destroy Sitka, but the Russians won eventually and rebuilt under the direction of Ivan Kuskov, Alexander Baranof's aide and bookkeeper. Kuskov was later in charge of the construction at Fort Ross, California, which is why there are similarities in the construction.

Captain William "Billy" Moore, founder of Skagway and discoverer of the White Pass, built this cabin in 1887. His claim to the land upon which the town of Skagway was built was largely ignored by the miners and stampeders who forcibly removed Moore from his property. Frank Reid, a surveyor, and others moved Moore's cabin, and it was many years after Skagway and its wild ways had nearly disappeared before his rights were established in court. Reid later killed Skagway's most infamous citizen, Randolph "Soapy" Smith, in a gunfight and died from wounds received in the fight. Moore, a ship's captain, became wealthy not from his land, but from his sawmill on the Skagway flats that provided most of the lumber for the boom town.

This information has value to today's log builder and clarifies some of the reasons for building as we've advised. Besides the similarities of construction that could be expected if one man supervised the Russian-American Company construction efforts, which was not always the case, there seems to have existed a "technical library" that the Russian-American Company assembled and placed in each of its outposts. Problems associated with construction and agriculture were among the subjects covered, apparently originally designed for the developing colonies in Siberia. McKenzie offers the following anecdote:

About 1950 a man came into Fort Ross and told of finding a pile of large, leather-bound books with the letters R.A.K. stamped on each, with the text all in Russian. He retrieved only one book from where he found the pile, in the San Francisco Dump! In a dozen tries I failed to locate him later. Such books may yet be found in Alaska or Siberia, and would account for the similarity in construction.

I contacted several rare book dealers, but none had any knowledge of such a collection of books, though one did find a small reference to an 1864 work that translates as *Information on Material for Buildings and Forts in the Colonies.* Perhaps, as McKenzie hopes, additional publicity will shed light on these lost volumes.

The Russian example of building well with logs was lost on those who rushed north for gold in 1898. Although cabin building was no secret to many of them, gold fever did not allow time for building quality cabins. A man doesn't need a topnotch cabin to spend one winter on a drainage waiting for the spring thaw. Most cabins were crudely built, had sod roofs and packed-dirt (mud, most of the year) floors, and stood barely long enough to keep the builder dry and warm. Fire, flood, permafrost, and shifting claims doomed many; rot got the rest. Although many picture books of Alaska feature photos entitled "Rustic

This old log building built with square saddle notches is now the Chitina Bar, headquarters for the hordes that descend on the small town each summer to dip-net for salmon.

Alaska cabin of the gold-rush era," such cabins are usually only 40 to 50 years old. Most of the original gold-rush cabins are long faded from sight.

In 1935, when the government, seeking solutions to the Depression, relocated 202 poverty-stricken families from the Midwest to Alaska, the reliance on Alaskan forest products continued. The Matanuska Valley colony was set up to become Alaska's agriculture center. By government and community effort, log homes and barns were built on the land allocated to each family. Some of these log homes were built in grand style, though most were not; only a few of the original barns and homes remain.

One of the most interesting of these survivors is the United Protestant Church (Presbyterian) still in use in Palmer. Built in the winter of 1936–37, the 3,700-square-foot church, called "the church of a thousand trees," was constructed under the guidance of the Reverend Bert J. Bingle by colony volunteers. Constructed with two 15-foot-by-30-foot wings, the building is a blend of horizontal and vertical logs with many interior highlights. The roof over the 32-foot-by-84-foot main portion of the church is supported by huge log

trusses. The chandeliers are made of log ends, and the birch pulpit is the original, built for the church in 1937. In front of the pulpit is a carved service table built by students at the then Sheldon Jackson Boarding Home in Sitka under the direction of the Reverend Earl Jackman. In 1975 the exterior of the church was sandblasted and the logs refinished.

From the late 1940s through the early 1960s, log building fell out of favor in Alaska and was replaced by more modern, or urban, styles of construction. In a rush to sweep away the vestiges of the "frontier," a "just-like-in-the Lower-48" syndrome prevailed.

Fortunately, in the early 1970s, a renaissance of the art of log building began, and by 1980 it had blossomed into a veritable boom in interest and in construction of log buildings. Logsmiths, using either the scribe-fit or the two-sided natural log technique, had demonstrated that log cabins need not be crude or rustic affairs, but rather could be built to compete favorably with any modern architecture. The atavistic appeal of the Alaska "frontier" lifestyle did the rest. Now, most logsmiths can't keep up with the demand.

This photo was taken in about 1910. The house, built of stick logs in Eagle, is now covered with siding, but still stands. The unidentified soldier was probably from nearby Fort Egbert. (Courtesy of the Eagle Historical Society)

No home is complete without furnishings and the basic accouterments for day-to-day living. A log cabin, especially one without power and heated solely with wood, needs a few special accessories not standard to conventional urban housing.

Log cabins in summer, without heat, can be quite cool, but fire up the stove to cook and the room temperature soon rises to an uncomfortable level. The whole idea of good log construction is to fit the logs tightly together to keep out the cold and seal in the heat. A good cabin, then, is warm in winter but cool in summer.

Vents — Screen doors and fancy crank-open windows aren't readily available to many bush people, so a common practice is to cut small vent openings in the gables just under the ridgepole at both ends of the cabin. At the pull of a long cord, the vent doors open or close on metal or leather hinges. Usually the vents are screened to prevent the entry of squirrels and to keep out summer's hordes of flying insects. The vents can be operated at will, summer or winter, or left open when the cabin is vacant for extended periods to prevent mildew damage to the interior. Because of heat loss and frost buildup, simple vents are not recommended but are a common bush solution to lack of adequate cross ventilation.

Fireplaces — Nowhere in this book will you find fireplaces or fireplace designs. This is not an oversight. In my view, an open fireplace has no real

Accouterments and Outbuildings

*Harold Eastwood's bush retreat—
the essence of the Alaska dream for
many—has the quintessential Alaskan
cache, complete with caribou antlers,
pole-and-sod roof, and dogsled.*

This Fisher Baby Bear nicely heats a house built by Brian Forbes; note the insulated stovepipe that extends up through the roof.

practical value in a cabin or northern home. Without doubt, a fireplace is a remarkably inefficient heating device and altogether too expensive to warrant construction. In a fireplace, the amount of wood fuel determines the heat output. The abundance of oxygen makes the fireplace quite inefficient, with as much as 90% of the heat from the burning fuel rushing up the chimney along with the excess available room air. For example, a friend of mine, Marty Rinio, built his first home with logs and, picturing the Alaska dream house, put his multiple talents to work creating a beautiful rock fireplace. One winter day, when the temperature was about -40° in his community of North Pole, I stopped by for a visit. "I'd build a fire in the fireplace for you," he laughed, "but it'd get cold in here."

Rinio's experience is not unique. In addition, most fireplaces frost up in cold weather when not in use. Also, fireplaces are hazardous unless used with a fire screen. Spruce, a common Alaska firewood, pops and spits as the pitch ignites, throwing sparks and embers in any direction. A spark screen is a must for safe fireplace use. Wood stoves are much, much more efficient than fireplaces.

Woodboxes — A drawback to the use of any wood-burning heating device, however, is the mess caused by the transfer of wood indoors and ashes outdoors. A woodbox near the stove, but far enough away not to pose a fire hazard, is a must. An ideally situated stove is located a minimal distance from an outside door with access over an easy-to-clean floor covering. Firewood is dirty, with bark, soil, sawdust, and wood chips accompanying each armload. A woodbox located just inside the door will minimize but not eliminate the dirt problem. I've seen several cabins with a wood door cut into the wall near the stove. All you had to do was open the small door and load firewood directly into the woodbox by the stove. Ashes can also be boxed and handed out the same opening. A wood door minimizes and localizes the mess created by firewood, but can create a frost and draft problem if the door doesn't seal properly.

I've also heard of two other problems related to wood doors. In one instance, a Fairbanks couple went off to visit friends for a few days, and when they came home, they found their locked cabin burglarized, the thieves having gained entrance through the 18-inch-tall wood door. Another time, a bush family returned from a sojourn to find that a black bear had taken up residence in their cabin, also by entering through the wood door. In both cases deadbolt locks remedied the problem, though each reported continuing frost problems in winter.

A massive cedar log house overlooking Kachemak Bay has a dumbwaiter-like affair that, at the push of a button, comes up through a concealed trap door in the floor, delivering a load of firewood from the cords stacked in the basement. The ashes go out the same way, thus protecting the carpets and furnishings. Since many of us haven't the time or money to invest in gadgetry like this, no matter how ideal, a simpler solution is to build a firewood box on wheels so that the firewood can be rolled into the house and the ashes rolled out. The simplest such device I've seen was an old rectangular gasoline crate with two wheels attached to one bottom edge, and a leather strap for a handle on the top. Not fancy, but it worked; the woodbox rolled outside to be filled and then back into place near the stove without leaving a trail of debris across the floor.

Stove Accessories—Cleaning the ashes from a stove can create an awful mess, especially since the slightest disturbance will send fine ash billowing all over the room. A fire poker, broom or brush, and long-handled ash shovel are standard accessories for any wood stove, but to be effective tools, the ashes still must be handled carefully to prevent undue mess. An additional accessory of value is a plastic spray bottle full of water. Spray the ashes inside the stove so that they stick together as they are shoveled out. Also, by wetting down the layers of ash, you extinguish any dangerous hot coals.

The fire protection sources I contacted during the preparation of this book indicated that the single most important stove accessory is a top-quality fire extinguisher. One fire marshal pointed out that a speedy application of chemical extinguisher can nip a fire in the bud and save a house, especially a log house, since, as he put it, "They're essentially piles of firewood someone's living in." In the bush it's wise to keep a barrel full of water and/or a box of dirt around just for fire emergencies. In winter, an outdoor rain barrel freezes solid and is of little use, so never allow the inside water barrel or cistern to get less than half empty.

Ladder—Most bush cabins have a ladder propped up against the side of the cabin next to the chimney. Not only does the ladder allow you to climb on the roof for regular chimney maintenance and inspection, but it also serves as a constant reminder of the task.

A ladder doesn't need to be fancy, just functional—not rickety. A ladder can be built of most any material, scrap log pieces, dimensional lumber, or even pipe sections fit together. I've seen ladders made of peeled black-spruce poles that serve as both a functional tool and a decorative feature. (Well, if you've got to look at it all the time, you might as well look at something worth

The roof line on the main lodge at Chena Hot Springs extends not only to protect the logs, but to cover the drying firewood. Note the cedar shingle roof and that the roof support logs are braced. You can never have too much wood cut or drying.

Harold Eastwood's cabin is a good example of the possibilities when a craftsman decides to create something unique, yet traditional: A pole roof covers the porch, a welded trap works as the door handle, the spruce reclining chair invites the visitor to relax, and the chair hewn from a stump suggests that a conversation might soon develop; note the pegging in the chair.

looking at.) No matter the design, the ladder should be kept up against the cabin or close by, not off in a shed or on loan to neighbors. In an emergency, a ladder does no good if it is miles away. Make sure the ladder is firmly supported and usable at a moment's notice. A ladder hooked over the peak is a permanent feature of many homes with steep-pitched roofs. For many cheechakos, this discussion of ladders as a significant feature of a northern home might seem a little strange, but the reality of life in the bush where there is no fire protection makes this item indispensable.

Furniture—Although the type of furniture used has little to do with the appeal of a cabin interior, the way the furnishings are used does. In most cases, an interior laid out in such a way as to show off the logwork, rather than hide it behind cupboards, partitions, Sheetrock, and the like, turns a log house into a home. When people speak of log homes being warm, they don't mean the ambient air temperature, but rather the cozy, good feeling emanating from the place.

Log homes are definitely synergistic, and you come away from a good log home with memories. For me, besides the appreciation for the log handicraft itself, it's the little things I remember best. The antique 1890s saloon mirror in a modern log house in Fairbanks; the towel rack made from hand-whittled spruce limbs in a kitchen in Cooper Landing; a burl table in a small cabin in McGrath; the natural spruce molding used around the windows and doors in a cabin on Edgemire Pond; log-end lamps on either side of a plush couch in a $100,000 log house in Anchorage; a Roy Smith–built rocker in a Homer place; a hanging lamp artfully crafted from driftwood in a log mansion near Ketchikan.

Recently I strolled through a cabin on the edge of a pond offering a spectacular view of Mount Drum. The arctic entry is rather dark and stepped down from the main part of the house, so that when the door opens to the main room, you look first out the big window to the mountains. The semidark entryway has low shelves for boots, high

Roy Smith, a logsmith and builder of unique, quality log furniture, uses a drawshave and shaving horse to peel a black-spruce pole. His workshop is complete and orderly.

Gary Rogers, a man of many skills—
commercial fisherman, air charter pilot,
heavy-equipment operator, and log
·builder—built his own log home and
some of the furniture, such as this
half-log bench.

The techniques of scribing aren't just for
houses—this unique scribe-fit picnic
table was crafted by Brian Forbes.

shelves for mittens and hats, and pegs for coats, effectively containing the usual clutter. One wall has storage shelves and in the corner, next to the main door, is the woodbox. All the pegs and shelf supports are hand-whittled spruce and the shelves are made of milled birch.

Inside the cabin, whittled pegs are spaced around the stove for drying clothes. All the door handles in this cabin are made of pieces of shed moose and caribou antler, as is a toothbrush rack that hangs above the counter. Like many cabins, this one has a tie log, but instead of a vertical post from the tie log to the ridgepole, the builder has fit a peeled burl for support. I suppose the most distinctive feature is that the cabin has running water. (By running water I don't mean that you "run out and get it" each time you need it.) Built into a birch-board cupboard over the sink is a 30-gallon fiberglass-sealed plywood box that can be filled through a trap door on the outside. Pipe and a faucet allow gravity feed to the sink below. Although this isn't all that unique, since many bush cabins have similar designs, it's just another little thing that makes the entire cabin special.

I like those hand-whittled pegs, but another good idea is Shaker pegs. These are milled pegs and knobs shaped like those the New England Shakers used on cabinets and furniture. Simple, but in tune with a handcrafted home.

Root Cellar—You may not have a need for an actual root cellar, but when the power goes out or you're away for an extended period of time, a well-insulated root cellar offers a safe storage place for breakables and items that otherwise would be ruined by freezing. Too, in areas where the corner store is miles away, the cellar can serve as a natural even-temperature pantry. I saw one root cellar that not only served the original function but doubled as a wine cellar, pantry, and storage area for drinking water. Even on the coldest days, without heat in the cabin, the temperature in that cellar stays an even 44° to 48° Fahrenheit.

It's the little things that make each log home unique. The late Cecil Rhode, a longtime Alaskan outdoorsman, built his first home on Kenai Lake in 1937, and later built a larger home on the same site. Some of the interesting finishing touches in the two homes include a cottonwood chair, a coat hook on the back of a door, and this paper towel holder—both made from spruce limbs.

Jay Hammond's place at Lake Clark has been added onto over the years and now boasts several practical outbuildings and additions, including this unique log bridge built by Monroe Robinson in 1979. The logs originally had an upward bow in them and have since settled level.

Monroe Robinson and John Bronson built this greenhouse in 1980, which is heated by a wood stove.

Hammond himself built this unique fish smokehouse in 1978. With its removable plywood panels it can also be used as a screened-in, ventilated meat-hanging building. (All photos by Monroe Robinson)

Cooler—Another simple item of value, especially if your cabin is in the bush away from power, is a free-air cooler. Attached to a shaded wall or up under the porch overhang, a simple screened-over box designed to allow free air flow and keep insects out will keep perishables cool in summer. In winter you can use it for storing ski waxes or small necessities. Caution: A cooler sometimes isn't practical, because bears, black bears in particular, and other critters have a fondness for ripping things up, with screened-over boxes containing dairy products a particular target.

Woodsheds—There are two or three small outbuildings that go with most any log house: a woodshed, a cache, and an outhouse. A good woodshed is of first concern. Some friends have one that seems ideal at their lakeside cabin. Large logs set vertically into the ground support horizontal log beams. The beams support a trussed, steep-pitched roof. Stove-length sections of wood can be stacked between the vertical uprights, as well as inside the shed, to a height of about 8 feet. The open sides allow good air circulation for drying, while the overhang prevents rain from wetting the wood. Some woodsheds have solid log walls, and others are similar post-and-beam, but sided with rough-cut lumber. No matter where your cabin is, Anchorage, Bettles, or Southeast Alaska, if you heat with wood, you need a woodshed.

Caches—Although caches may seem rather gimmicky to modern Alaskans, since they so often have been rendered quaint by artists, photographers, and gift shop owners, a cache serves as a useful, safe storage area for food and gear. If nothing else, a cache should contain a supply of emergency clothing in case of cabin fire. All too tragically one hears of families burned out on an arctic night, lucky to have escaped in their nightclothes. In the bush at subzero temperatures, such an event can prove fatal. Having good warm clothes in a safe accessible place, such as your cache, could save a life.

I know of several persons who first

Pete Buist, a Fairbanks resident and trapper, uses his cache as an outdoor freezer in the winter. Note the whitefish hanging under the cache—food for his dog team.

This round-log cache is in Nenana. Note that the log ends are trimmed in a slant toward the base, rather than flaring out at the base, an excellent design. The flashing around the legs is to keep climbing animals out.

Paul Smith, in the red plaid shirt, mixes concrete for the slab in the garage he built of two-sided logs for Buster Allen's home on the Kenai River.

There are many unique features in the cabin at Byers Lake, including the amazing scribe-fit burled log at left — the burl has even been cut to form a small ledge. On the porch, above, the burls have been halved for tables and the railing has been mortised into the end projection of the wall log. Logwork by Dave Johnston, Pete Robinson, and George Menard.

Although a rough lumber outhouse may look cold and uncomfortable to the city dweller, it becomes a real treasure when the pipes freeze. And outhouses need not be stinky or cold, or dark. Harold Eastwood sawed off a burl, hollowed it out, and fit it with a Styrofoam seat—warm regardless of the outside temperature— and then topped it with a burl lid. (Above) Roger Cline's electrically lit outhouse is reached by crossing a bridge.

built their cache, then later, usually the next summer, put up their cabin. One couple I know prepared the building site, cut and piled the logs for a cabin, then split and stacked a cord of firewood. Next, they hauled in enough logs to build a good cache to store their tools and camp over the winter. The following spring they started construction and in one month's time had their cabin roofed over. One other person I know went at it in grand style, building a cache big enough to live in while the main cabin went up. Also, though he didn't say so, he actually perfected his building technique on that 10-foot-by-12-foot cache. He said the only drawback to living 12 feet off the ground was remembering to watch his footing when stepping outside at night.

Most caches aren't as grandiose as that windowed, log highrise. A good 5-foot-by-5-foot cache, on posts 10 feet to 12 feet off the ground, is quite serviceable. Flattened metal cans or flashing nailed around the legs prevents access by climbing animals. Squirrels and martens, however, are capable leapers and can easily gain access from nearby trees. Ideally, a cache should stand in a clearing, but away from the house so that a disaster won't menace it as well. In black bear country, a cache, even with metal nailed to the legs, sometimes serves as nothing more than a Junglegym. Blacks climb amazingly well and are so strong that their claws can penetrate thin sheet metal. The most critter-proof cache I ever saw was built on stout 12-foot log uprights, with 55-gallon drums with the ends cut out placed down over the tops of the uprights before the cache platform itself was constructed. Any climbing animal shinnying up those posts will quickly find itself in a barrel with nowhere to go but down.

Outhouses—Finally, although I suppose all the sanitation experts and urban consultants from Juneau, Anchorage, Fairbanks, and points south will protest, I believe an outhouse should go with every home. I admit this isn't feasible in many areas and is totally out of the question for apartment and condominium dwellers, and I'm not advocating outdoor facilities over indoor

plumbing. What I am advocating, however, is an outhouse in addition to indoor plumbing. Frozen pipes and broken sewer lines are a fact of northern life. Such things happen in Anchorage as well as in Talkeetna. What then? If you have an outhouse, the hassle is minimized.

I've seen several fine-quality log outhouses. All the openings were screened and the logs were tightly fit. Some were carpeted, others were heated and lighted electrically. One of the most unique outhouses I've seen was built by Harold Eastwood. The throne was a hollowed-out, slabbed-off burl. The lid was a hinged piece of burl with a natural handle. The seat itself was Styrofoam. It was an

attractive, clean, and odor-free privy.

Perhaps, in this day and age, it's rather iconoclastic to advocate the building of an outhouse when anything less than indoor plumbing is considered substandard. But what is a family to do when the pipes or wellhead freezes up? Outhouses—well-designed and kept clean—are quite problem-free in most areas, though they can pose a sanitation problem in areas with permafrost.

Although municipal ordinances may prevent you from building an outhouse, a woodshed and cache aren't prohibited. Also, you can envision the need for a guest cabin, or workshop, perhaps a sauna, or garage, or how about a. . . .

After skiing on a cold winter's night, or after a long hike on the summer tundra, a sauna relaxes and refreshes.

t'd be tough to choose the number-one rule for the bush, but "If it isn't your cabin, don't use it" and "If it isn't yours, don't take it" rank right up there with "If you use it, replace it" and "Take care with fire."

Most bush Alaskans have one great fear, other than cabin fire, and that is to come home from a trip and find their cabin used, abused, ravaged, or vandalized. The main crimes seem to be looting and misuse of property. A common misconception of many urban Alaskans, as dramatized by the following incident, is that the bush is full of abandoned cabins.

Jim Okonek is a mild-mannered, retired military man. With the aid of his family, he built a beautiful log cabin on a bluff overlooking a wilderness lake. Except for a friend's old cabin nearby and one newer cabin owned by a longtime friend, no one else lives in the area.

One day Jim was hard at work around the cabin when two planes flew over. After circling a bit they landed and taxied up to the shore in front of the old cabin. Minutes later Jim heard the bear boards being pulled off the door and windows, and saw the people enter the cabin. Jim's friend had asked him to keep an eye on the place, so he went over and politely told the intruders, who were busily engaged in moving the cabin contents out onto the porch, that they'd have to leave because this was private property. When they said they had every right to fish the lake and stay in the cabin, Jim welcomed them to the fishing but said again that the cabin was private property and they couldn't use it. For a moment things got tense, but eventually the trespassers threw their stuff in the planes and took off, leaving

14

Bush Cabin Etiquette

A bush cabin by lamplight—
warm and cozy and inviting.
The Alaska dream alive. (Tom Klein)

This old cabin and cache in the Brooks Range may appear to be abandoned, but they belong to a mining claim owner. Buildings and their contents are private property, and so-called souvenir hunters are really thieves.

Jim the task of replacing the cabin contents and reboarding up the door and windows.

Put the shoe on the other foot. What if Jim Okonek took a notion to go into Anchorage for supplies and, unable to finish his shopping, decided to "camp out" in the first empty "abandoned" home he came to? Most likely, if he didn't get shot by the returning owner, he'd be arrested and thrown in the slammer.

Just remember, no matter how old, rundown, or dilapidated a cabin might look, it belongs to somebody and should be treated as private property. Old mining cabins and camps dating from the 1920s and 1930s may look as though they're abandoned, but in reality they still may be used each mining season. You might see old relics inside, but woe to the person some grizzled miner catches hauling any of his stuff away.

No bush cabin dweller objects to someone using his cabin in time of emergency. When a plane goes down, survivors' only hope might be the chance encounter of a bush cabin, with food and firewood inside.

It used to be an old rule of the trail that anyone could use any cabin as long as they left behind a haunch of caribou or slab of bacon, a pile of firewood, and a bucket of water or pot of ice on the stove. In the days of snowshoe and dog-team travel, this simple rule might have meant the difference between life and death. Nowadays such common-sense rules go largely ignored, to the loss of all involved.

Late one winter night a few years back, with the temperature -20°, I returned home to my cabin to find that someone, an Anchorage surveyor it turned out, had stayed in my cabin while I was gone and used every single stick of firewood. Every piece, including some birch I had set aside for carving. Can you imagine what it'd be like to get in late one frigid arctic night, legs wet from falling through the ice, in desperate need of fire, and have no firewood?

For years, locks on bush cabin doors were unheard of. Not anymore. After that incident, I started locking my door.

Ken Cassity, a lawyer by trade who moved to the bush to build a log home, takes a break from his dogged attempts to teach himself to play the banjo. Time in the bush allows for such pursuits and for reading—"a broadening of educational experience," he says. Unlike some bush dwellers, or bush rats as they are sometimes called, Ken is a kind, gracious, and welcoming host. However, never approach an inhabited bush cabin without first shouting a warning.

Building the Alaska Log Home

Some folks leave their bush cabins unlocked, with a notice placed in a prominent place welcoming visitors, with the only stipulation being the users replace whatever they use. One cabin has this notice on the door:

> *Welcome. Though humble, this cabin is home to me, my wife, and two children. It's all we have. If you are lost or in dire straits, you are welcome to anything we have. We ask nothing in return.*
>
> *However, if you're vacationing or just passing through, and must (?) stay here, please use the work shed, it has stove and wood. We only ask that you replace what you use, and treat this place as you would have us treat your home.*

Other old trail rules are as practical today as in the old days. Old-timers would never walk up and knock on a cabin door. They'd stand back away and shout a hello or greeting. Most would especially be cautious around cabins inhabited by people they didn't know. This is a good idea today, too. Hearing leaves crunching on the trail close by or boards creaking on the porch step start some folks reaching for a rifle. Human visitors can be an uncommon happening in the bush, and the usual, and more unwanted, visitor could be a grizzly or black bear. Those inside have no way of knowing who or what's out there, so a wise visitor makes his presence known in advance. Also, occupants of remote cabins may not be prepared for company; a loud hello gives them a chance to get things together. One-room cabins function as washroom, bedroom, living room, and kitchen, all at once, so don't knock without prior warning.

Nothing is more anticipated in the bush than visits with invited guests. Most bush folk are happy just to see the smiling faces of friends or relatives, but a visitor with a bag of fresh vegetables and fruit under an arm is doubly welcome. In the bush there aren't any neighborhood stores, so fresh stuff is a prized gift. There's little else that is more appreciated.

Mail is very important to bush people and some might want visitors to bring in the mail, too. But it would be wise to check on that first, since some people can be quite fussy and want their mail delivered the regular way.

Most bush folks don't have much money. Chances are they're trying to get out of the cash economy as much as possible and can't afford to feed mobs of visitors. A wise and true friend will ask before showing up for the weekend and, at least, bring some extra food and supplies.

There's a lot of work that goes into living in the bush: hauling water and logs, splitting firewood, and maintenance of the trail or airstrip and cabin. Bush folk laugh when city friends ask, "But what do you do to keep busy out there?" There's always work and daily chores to get done. Visitors aren't expected to help, but any help offered is most likely to be accepted. No one minds an extra pair of hands to haul water or wood. Do what you can, but always ask before you use someone's

A young man and woman spent a winter in this tiny V-plank-corner cabin near the Tanana River, miles from any neighbors and with only their dogs for company. The one-room cabin served as their kitchen, dining room, living room, and bedroom.

tools. I used to cringe whenever anybody picked up an ax or maul to "help" out. I couldn't help but think of how far it was to a doctor, or where I could get a replacement for the maul handle should it break. Later, I took to hiding the axes from helpful visitors.

There're myriad ways to be of help around a bush cabin, but many bush folk have pretty ingrained ways of doing things, so always ask first. It might seem fine to you, but your better way might not seem so to the cabin owner. Don't fill lanterns or kerosene lamps unless specifically asked to do so, and you know for sure you've the right fuel. Kerosene and Blazo (white gas) both are lamp fuels, but work in different ways in different lamps. Kerosene burns nice and slow in a glass lamp, but Blazo turns it into a molotov cocktail.

Conservation is the key word in bush living. Bush folk don't excessively use or waste anything, including water. Remember how thick the ice in the water hole was, or how far it had to be carried? Go light on everything, for chances are, every item had to be flown, mushed, snow-machined, or backpacked in quite a distance.

Bush folk owe something to urbanites, too. Just because one lives in a remote valley or along some wilderness river doesn't mean that that person owns all that surrounds. I know a fellow on Wood River who routinely blocks all the sandbars and airstrips in his area to keep out everyone else. That's public land, owned by all, and legally open to all. He has no right. Such abuses occur elsewhere, too. No one says that bush folk have to be wildly accepting of vacationers or passersby, but that doesn't mean hostile behavior, exemplified by the get-out-of-our-country attitude, is correct either. Master woodsman and trapper Joe Delia of Skwentna is an example of one person who bends over backward to make people welcome, offering help to any who need it. His attitude is in stark contrast to those like the Wood Riverite, who do nothing but broaden the gap between rural and urban Alaskans.

No matter how simple or crude, a cabin in the bush is home and castle. This one has upright corners, pole roof, and logs chinked with moss. For want of proper waterproofing, the cache fell down in a few years.

The Alaska Dream. Everyone, it seems, at least once in a while dreams of having a log cabin in the high bush: a place to get away from it all, share the natural world with just family, no neighbors, only the wild birds and animals for company. What Alaskan, even the greenest cheechako, hasn't envisioned some pristine place, a cabin on the lakeshore, fish dimpling the waters, bears prowling the woods, and moose calling in the thicket?

Sit back and picture yourself in that cabin on a wintry night, cold and snow piled high on the outside, but the warm glow of oil lamps and wood heat inside. Romantic? You bet, but who hasn't come to Alaska with just a part of that dream tucked away in the back of their mind?

For some folks, the Alaska dream centers around a bush retreat—a place to escape from the modern world. A warm, snug place in the high bush is the epitome of their dreams. This is a small trapline cabin at Crooked Teapot in the Mentasta Mountains. (Sue Entsminger)

For many, it's just a dream, though perhaps a dream that keeps the day-to-day grind from becoming too burdensome. Some folks do live the dream, thus giving spark to those who will try and to those who will always only dream. These folks know all the reality, as well as romantic fantasies, of building and living in your own log cabin in the woods. R. Buckminster Fuller, on one of his trips here, called Alaska the "land of insurmountable opportunity," and he was right, of course. Where else in America these days can a person do what can be done in Alaska? Live the lifestyle of your own choosing, make your own way, build a log cabin in the woods? Nowhere else, that's where.

The reality of living isolated in the bush the year round discourages most folks, while for others, that lifestyle was never part of *their* Alaska Dream. Maybe they picture a weekend retreat, or just a slice of the Alaska pie-in-the-sky to go along with other more

15

The Alaska Dream

For others, the Alaska dream may be a not-so-remote log home. The J. C. Quast home, built by Tom McColl at Auke Bay in 1934, sits not far from the road into Juneau. This beautiful, flowered retreat stands in stark contrast to the bustle of Alaska's capital city.

Building the Alaska Log Home

The home of Jack and Diana Greene in Eagle, Alaska, may look like most any other modern two-sided-log house, but it is not. Jack, once a research scientist and engineer with the National Bureau of Standards, has created a most unique home. Although the corners appear to be butt and run, the logs are actually joined at the corners with a blind, semi-dovetail notch of Jack's own design. The windows are quadruple-paned and the air spaces between are vented to the outside to equalize the pressure as the atmospheric pressure changes. Vents in the gables, which are almost identical to the trapdoor style found in old sourdough cabins, open and close with a pull on a black thread. A dumbwaiter-like device in the kitchen area drops down a shaft into the permafrost below the building—a natural refrigerator and storage area. The basement contains a complete metal shop and wood shop, powered by a huge bank of batteries. Jack is presently working on a heat collector that will sit next to the wood stove in the basement. Then, when the Greenes are away and the wood stove is out, the collector will radiate heat, keeping the house warm until they return. Jack and Diana, a doctor of philosophy in classical literature, seek what Jack calls "a quality bush life with couth."

This building was constructed in Homer, then trucked to the author's site at Denali Park for reassembly in late winter. A hand winch was used to move the logs from the roadside to the site.

conventional life pursuits. Central to the Alaska Dream, and the myriad variations, is the log cabin. A log house just shouts *ALASKA!*

The dream of a log home isn't beyond the realm of possibility, even for those of limited income. You can build your own . . . it is possible. Logwork, as we've shown, is no great secret; you only have to know a few basic principles, own some tools, and have the desire to work hard and persevere. And if you can't build for yourself, or could but don't have the time, there's a growing cadre of logsmiths, dedicated to preserving the old skills and improving upon them, who will build for you. They may not say such things but in each logsmith is the desire to create something beautiful, useful, and unique.

Something that blends with the natural world, instead of standing in spite of it. Logwork doesn't come cheap, for there's a part of the builder in every log structure. It's the sweat, toil, and sometimes blood that make log cabins unique one-of-a-kind homes.

It is this quality that fits log homes into the Alaska Dream, with the log cabin a big part of it. Part of a frontier mythology? You bet, but what's wrong with that?

Bob Weeden, the gifted biologist, no, biologist-poet, at the University of Alaska Fairbanks, once presented a paper that dealt in part with the frontier mythology. He said: "In a very real sense, what I am proposing is not only a milieu for Alaskans but an opportunity for the world. The world needs an

embodiment of the frontier mythology, the sense of horizons unexplored, the mystery of uninhabited miles. It needs a place where wolves stalk the strand lines in the dark, because a land that can produce a wolf is a healthy, robust, and perfect land. The world desperately needs a place to stand under a bright auroral curtain on a winter's evening, in awe of the cosmic cold and silence. But more than these things the world needs to know that there is a place where men live amidst a balanced interplay of the goods of technology and the fruits of Nature. Unless we can prove that a modern society can thrive in harmony with the land, the bits of wilderness we salvage in Alaska will be nothing more than curious artifacts in the sad museum of mankind."

The original log home of the late Cecil Rhode and his wife, Helen. They lived in this 16-foot-by-24-foot cabin on Kenai Lake for 25 years. Then they took this cabin down, log by log, and reassembled it here a few hundred feet from their new main house, which they built on the original site. See also pages 26–27 and 137.

Lynn Miille built this vertical-log home for his family in Eagle.

Logsmith Roger Cline built this log house in Homer in the traditional trapper, or sourdough, style.

The O. G. Simpson home near Bean Creek built by Dick Quinn.

Derek Stonorov and Roy Smith helped
Paul Budge build this home on the road
east of Homer. It boasts quality logwork,
framed gables, and a covered porch. The
interior is warm and inviting because the
Budges have worked hard to fill it with
art, good books, and things that reflect
their interests. Roy Smith's furniture looks
right at home here.

Anchorage—*Built in 1954, the visitors center was Lee A. Cole's first public building in Alaska. With its scribe-fit logs and sod roof, it is probably the most-photographed log structure in Alaska. Another Cole-built building in Anchorage is the Peanut Farm Lounge, shown on page 31.*

Public Buildings

Kenai—*The Holy Assumption of the Virgin Mary Russian Orthodox Church was built in 1895. The logs are actually fit with dovetail notches (see page 41) that have since been covered with siding.*

Anchorage—*The Unitarian Universalists Fellowship, at 602 West 10th, is a contrast of the old and the new.*

Homer—*The Salty Dawg Saloon on the Homer Spit is one of only two original Homer buildings to survive both the 1907 fire and the 1964 earthquake.*

Palmer—*The visitors center was built in 1967 for the Alaska Purchase Centennial by Jimmy Hitchcock, a professional logsmith who also teaches three-sided-log building. The center is located at South Valley Way and East Firewood Avenue and houses a small museum in the basement.*

Palmer—*(Top) The United Protestant Church (Presbyterian), also known as "the church of a thousand trees," was built in 1936 by the Depression-era farmers who were shipped to the Matanuska Valley by the federal government and given land to farm. Originally a mission project of the Presbyterian Church, it is the only original colony church still in regular use.* (Courtesy of Henry Guinnotte)

(Left) Interior of the church.

Talkeetna—*This climbers shelter was built for K-2 Aviation by Chris and Arthur Mannix; post and beam construction with a single truss supporting roof.*

Copper Center—*The Chapel on the Hill, near Copper Center on the Richardson Highway, suffers from weathering and looks older than it actually is. It was built in 1942 of round logs and joined with round notches.*

Tok—*The Burnt Paw Trading Post, at the junction of the Alaska and Glenn Highways, was built by Bill Arpino in the winter of 1977–78. The two-sided-log building is one of the most-photographed log structures in Alaska, partly because Tok is the major overland point of entry to Alaska.*

Fairbanks—*The visitors center is at First Avenue and Cushman on the bank of the Chena River where a riverside marker indicates the end of the Alaska Highway. Built by Harold Herning, the building has a typical Alaska sod roof that has required additional external support.*

Fairbanks—*The National Electrical Contractors Association office was built in 1974 by the late Oscar Queen on the bank of the Chena River. The logs are two-sided, joined by round notches, and the sod roof is pure grass.*

Fairbanks—*These rental cabins, located at the junction of the Steese Highway and the Chena Hot Springs Road, were built in the traditional trapper style.*

Fairbanks—The dog mushers clubhouse at the Jeff Studdert Race Grounds off Farmers Loop Road was completed by master logsmith Jeff Harrison of Logweavers in Nenana. This building is state of the art in scribe-fit log construction. There are five purlins between the ridgepole and the caplog, and the settling spaces above the windows have been covered with framing and the log ends have been trimmed at varying lengths (below). Note that the roof line covers all the logwork. This is a good building to study.

Fairbanks—This cabin at Sixth and Noble was constructed of two-sided logs in 1973 by Jim Smith, Mike Stephenson, and me. We prefabricated most of the building on a lot out on Sheep Creek Road north of town and then reassembled it on the site. The construction went fast, but the neighbors complained about the noise of the chainsaws, especially early on Sunday mornings.

Building the Alaska Log Home

Fairbanks—*The Goldstream General Store in Goldstream Valley just north of Fairbanks was built in 1973 by Jim Smith with two-sided logs. Note the burl and diamond willow fitted into a rail on the porch; the log ends were cut with a chainsaw and worked over with an ax to display ax markings rather than chainsaw marks.*

Fairbanks—*Many old cabins, such as the brown and white V-plank-corner cabin from Prostitute's Line on Fourth Avenue in Fairbanks, have been moved and preserved at Alaskaland, a 44-acre historic park just off Airport Way. The sign on the cabin tells visitors that a fence once protected passersby from viewing the scenes of "lust and debauchery." Ironically, we now restore these old cabins and open them for public viewing.*

North Pole—*Radio station KJNP (King Jesus North Pole) broadcasts the Gospel to the North Country in several languages. The logs are three-sided and the low walls and low pitch of the roof are practical in this area of prolonged cold weather where the temperature sometimes drops to minus 50° or colder in the winter. The sod roof is all grass, but it does not cover all the logs—those protruding from under the roof line show evidence of water damage.*

College—*The University Community Presbyterian Church is built with three-sided logs and notched corners.*

Chena Hot Springs—*The Chena Hot Springs Lodge, a private resort open year-round, is located at the end of the Chena Hot Springs Road, just 60 miles from Fairbanks. The mineral hot springs were first reported in 1907 by the U.S. Geological Survey.*

Nenana—*This cabin was built near Clear and in 1972 moved to the Parks Highway near the Nenana River. The Tatlanika Gift Shop was built of three-sided logs in 1976.*

Nenana—*The visitors center, at the intersections of the George Parks Highway and A Street, was built by Carl Jauhola of Nenana. Nenana is located at the confluence of the Tanana and Nenana Rivers and is the home port of the tug and barge fleet that supplies the villages along the Yukon and Tanana Rivers during the summer.*

Cooper Landing—*The public library was built by me in 1983.*

Juneau—*The visitors center, a replica of the Davis house, was built under the direction of Bill Basinski, by a University of Alaska log building class and CETA workers as part of the city's centennial celebration in 1980. Basinski and his crew were true to historic detail—the logwork is crude but effectively scribe-fit. The original cabin was built in 1881 and served as a carpenter's shop, Juneau's first school, first church, and finally a brewery office before being razed in 1914 to make way for a hotel. The cabin takes its name from John and Frances Davis, who were married in 1892 during the cabin's tenure as a church. Basinski got his first logwork experience working for me. The bell tower has been removed due to water damage.*

Chilkoot Trail—*A rare day of sunshine at the State of Alaska Department of Natural Resources shelter cabin at Canyon City, on the Chilkoot Trail. With the exception of some Forest Service cabins, this is probably one of the most-used public cabins in Alaska.*

Dawson City, Yukon Territory—*Actor Tom Byrne, in the role of Robert W. Service—the Bard of the Klondike—in front of Service's original cabin in Dawson City. When first built, the cabin sat in a vast clearing caused or created by the construction demands of the Klondike stampeders.*

Summit Lake—*Coffee and gift shop at Summit Lake on the Kenai Peninsula, built by Jeff Harrison and Bill Kisken.*

I built this cabin for Will and Lurue Troyer in Cooper Landing. The true test of a builder's skills comes in winter when the cabin must withstand attacks of wind, cold, and snow. Happily, this little cabin has proved to be exceptionally warm and comfortable.

The Last Word

Logsmith. A misused word? A dictionary definition of *smith* reads in part: "noun. 1. A worker in metal. 2. A blacksmith. (Old English)." Thus *logsmith:* noun. 1. A colloquialism. A craftsman, a builder of quality log structures. Perhaps logwright would be more accurate: *wright:* noun. 1. A workman, a maker of something; used chiefly in combination: a wheelwright, boatwright, playwright.

Perhaps more accurate, but neither quite right. But in an important part of Alaska, the term *logsmith* has become common and is used to mean a person who builds with logs.

To all the logsmiths who helped with ideas and inspiration, and provided their time and support, thanks. Two winters of sitting at a desk are now finished. Time to go peel logs. . . .

Index

*Indicates illustration

About the author

Tom Walker has lived and worked in Alaska for over 30 years. A premier wildlife photographer and writer, his work appears in many publications including *Alaska, Outdoor Life* and *Field & Stream.* He is the author of several books, including *We Live in the Alaska Bush, Shadows on the Tundra,* and *Alaska's Wildlife.* He lives in a log cabin he built himself near the entrance to Denali National Park.